# Lecture Notes in Computer Science 13860

Founding Editors

Gerhard Goos
Juris Hartmanis

The series Lecture Notes in Computer Science (LNCS), including its subseries Lecture Notes in Artificial Intelligence (LNAI) and Lecture Notes in Bioinformatics (LNBI), has established itself as a medium for the publication of new developments in computer science and information technology research, teaching, and education.

LNCS enjoys close cooperation with the computer science R & D community, the series counts many renowned academics among its volume editors and paper authors, and collaborates with prestigious societies. Its mission is to serve this international community by providing an invaluable service, mainly focused on the publication of conference and workshop proceedings and postproceedings. LNCS commenced publication in 1973.

Raghunath Nambiar · Meikel Poess
Editors

# Performance Evaluation and Benchmarking

14th TPC Technology Conference, TPCTC 2022
Sydney, NSW, Australia, September 5, 2022
Revised Selected Papers

 Springer

*Editors*
Raghunath Nambiar
Advanced Micro Devices Inc.
Santa Clara, CA, USA

Meikel Poess
Oracle Corporation
Redwood City, CA, USA

ISSN 0302-9743          ISSN 1611-3349 (electronic)
Lecture Notes in Computer Science
ISBN 978-3-031-29575-1          ISBN 978-3-031-29576-8 (eBook)
https://doi.org/10.1007/978-3-031-29576-8

# Preface

The Transaction Processing Performance Council (TPC) is a non-profit organization established in August 1988. It focuses on developing industry standards for data-centric workloads and disseminating vendor-neutral performance data to industry. Over the years, the TPC has had a significant impact on the computing industry's use of industry-standard benchmarks. Vendors use TPC benchmarks to illustrate performance competitiveness for their existing products, and to improve and monitor the performance of their products under development. Many buyers use TPC benchmark results as points of comparison when purchasing new computing systems.

In 2022 the full members of TPC were: Actian; Alibaba; AMD; Boray Data; Cisco; Dell EMC Fujitsu; Hewlett Packard Enterprise; Hitachi; Huawei; IBM; Inspur; Intel; Lenovo; Microsoft; Nettrix; Nutanix; Nvidia; Oracle; Red Hat; Transwarp; TTA; and VMware. The Associate Members were: Tsinghua University; University of Coimbra, Portugal; China Academy of Information and Communications Technology; and Imec. Additional information is available at http://www.tpc.org/.

The information technology landscape is evolving at a rapid pace, challenging industry experts and researchers to develop innovative techniques for evaluation, measurement and characterization of complex systems. The TPC remains committed to developing new benchmark standards to keep pace with these rapid changes in technology. One vehicle for achieving this objective is the TPC's sponsorship of the Technology Conference Series on Performance Evaluation and Benchmarking (TPCTC) established in 2009. With this conference series, the TPC encourages researchers and industry experts to present and debate novel ideas and methodologies in performance evaluation, measurement, and characterization.

This book contains the proceedings of the 14th TPC Technology Conference on Performance Evaluation and Benchmarking (TPCTC 2022), held in conjunction with the 45th International Conference on Very Large Data Bases (VLDB 2022) in Sydney, Australia, on September 5–9, 2022. Over the years TPCTC has become an important forum for the performance benchmarking community. This year, out of twelve papers submitted, five papers were accepted with an average of four peer reviews. The proceedings also include two paper-based panel discussions by industry and research experts and an invited paper from the chairman of the TPC public relations committee for new initiatives in TPC.

The hard work and close cooperation of a number of people contributed to the success of this conference. We would like to thank the members of TPC and the organizers of VLDB 2022 for their sponsorship; the members of the Program Committee and Publicity

Committee for their support; and the authors and the participants who are the primary reason for the success of this conference.

Raghunath Nambiar
Meikel Poess

# TPCTC 2022 Organization

## General Chairs

| | |
|---|---|
| Raghunath Nambiar | AMD, USA |
| Meikel Poess | Oracle, USA |

## Program Committee

| | |
|---|---|
| Dippy Aggarwal | Intel, USA |
| Daniel Bowers | Gartner, USA |
| Michael Brey | Oracle, USA |
| Karthik Kulkarni | Infobell IT, India |
| Ajay Dholakia | Lenovo, USA |
| Dhabaleswar Panda | Ohio State University, USA |
| Tilmann Rabl | TU Berlin, Germany |
| Swapna Raj | Intel, USA |
| Reza Taheri | VMWare, USA |

## Publicity Committee

| | |
|---|---|
| Meikel Poess | Oracle, USA |
| Andrew Bond | Red Hat, USA |
| Paul Cao | HPE, USA |
| Gary Little | Nutanix, USA |
| Raghunath Nambiar | AMD, USA |
| Reza Taheri | VMware, USA |
| Michael Majdalany | L&M Management Group, USA |
| Forrest Carman | Owen Media, USA |
| Andreas Hotea | Hotea Solutions, USA |

## TPC Steering Committee

| | |
|---|---|
| Michael Brey (Chair) | Oracle, USA |
| Matthew Emmerton | IBM, USA |
| Jamie Reding | Microsoft, USA |

| Ken Rule | Intel, USA |
| Nicholas Wakou | Dell EMC, USA |

## TPC Technical Advisory Board

| Paul Cao | HPE |
| Matt Emmerton | IBM |
| Gary Little | Nutanix |
| Jamie Reding (Chair) | Microsoft, USA |
| Mike Brey | Oracle |
| Ken Rule | Intel, USA |
| Nicholas Wakou | Dell EMC, USA |

## TPC Technical Subcommittee Chairs

TPC-C: Jamie Reding, Microsoft, USA
TPC-H: Meikel Poess, Oracle, USA
TPC-E: Matthew Emmerton, IBM, USA
TPC-DS: Meikel Poess, Oracle, USA
TPC-DI: Meikel Poess, Oracle, USA
TPC-OSS: Andy Bond, VMware, USA
TPCx-HS: Tariq Magdon-Ismail, VMware, USA
TPCx-IoT: Meikel Poess, Oracle, USA
TPCx-BB: Rodrigo Escobar, Intel, USA
TPCx-AI: Hamesh Patel, Intel, USA
TPC-Pricing: Jamie Reding, Microsoft, USA
TPC-Energy: Paul Cao, HPE, USA

# Contents

# Pick & Mix Isolation Levels: Mixed Serialization Graph Testing

Jack Waudby[1]($\boxtimes$), Paul Ezhilchelvan[1], and Jim Webber[2]

[1] Newcastle University, School of Computing, Newcastle upon Tyne, England
{j.waudby2,paul.ezhilchelvan}@newcastle.ac.uk
[2] Neo4j, London, England
jim.webber@neo4j.com

**Abstract.** Concurrency control is an integral component in achieving high performance in many-core databases. Implementing serializable transaction processing efficiently is challenging. One approach, *serialization graph testing* (SGT) faithfully implements the *conflict graph theorem* by aborting only those transactions that would actually violate serializability (introduce a cycle), thus maintaining the required acyclic invariant. Alternative approaches, such as *two-phase locking*, disallow certain valid schedules to increase throughput, whereas SGT has the theoretically optimal property of accepting all and only conflict serializable schedules. Historically, SGT was deemed unviable in practice due to the high computational costs of maintaining an acyclic graph. Research has however overturned this historical view by utilising the increased computational power available due to modern hardware. Furthermore, a survey of 24 databases suggests that not all transactions demand conflict serializability but different transactions can perfectly settle for different, weaker isolation levels which typically require relatively lower overheads. Thus, in such a mixed environment, providing only the isolation level required of each transaction should, in theory, increase throughput and reduce aborts. The aim of this paper is to extend SGT for mixed environments subject to Adya's *mixing-correct theorem* and demonstrate the resulting performance improvement. We augment the YCSB benchmark to generate transactions with different isolation requirements. For certain workloads, *mixed serialization graph testing* can achieve up to a 28% increase in throughput and a 19% decrease in aborts over SGT.

**Keywords:** Databases · Concurrency Control · Weak Isolation · Serialization Graph Testing · Mixing-Correct Theorem · YCSB

## 1 Introduction

In a database management system (DBMS) concurrency control is responsible for ensuring the effects of concurrently executing transactions are isolated from each other, providing each with the illusion of running alone in the DBMS. This is captured by the correctness criteria *serializability*: if transactions are assumed to be individually correct, then an execution of transactions equivalent to a serial execution of the same transactions guarantees a correct DBMS state [1].

© The Author(s), under exclusive license to Springer Nature Switzerland AG 2023
R. Nambiar and M. Poess (Eds.): TPCTC 2022, LNCS 13860, pp. 1–16, 2023.
https://doi.org/10.1007/978-3-031-29576-8_1

Practically, DBMSs provide *conflict serializability* which is sufficient for guaranteeing serializability. Conflict serializability is based on *conflicts* between transactions. Two transactions conflict if both operate on the same data item and at least one operation is a write. A conflict imposes an order between transactions. If a serial execution can be found that respects the order imposed by conflicts then the execution is conflict serializable [1]. The goal of concurrency control protocols can be reformulated as allowing as many theoretically possible conflict serializable executions without reducing DBMS performance.

Implementing serializable transaction processing efficiently is difficult. The classical approach is *two-phase locking* (2PL) [2]. Such pessimistic approaches perform well under high contention, but suffer when workloads are dominated by read-only transactions. Optimistic approaches such as *timestamp ordering* and *optimistic concurrency control* [3] perform better in low contention workloads, but exhibit many unnecessary aborts when contention is high. However, each approach sacrifices a degree of concurrency to achieve higher throughput, approximating the complete space of conflict serializable executions. To illustrate this, consider concurrent transactions $T_W$ and $T_R$ both attempt to access a single data item, $x$. Assume $T_W$ holds a write lock on $x$, and $T_R$ wishes to read $x$. Under 2PL, depending on the deadlock detection strategy used, one of $T_W$ or $T_R$ will be aborted. Thus, discounting a perfectly legal conflict serializable schedule.

An alternative approach is *serialization graph testing* (SGT) [1,4]. In SGT, the scheduler maintains an acyclic *conflict graph* of the execution it controls. For each operation in a transaction, each conflict is determined and represented by an edge in the conflict graph; a cycle check is then performed before executing the operation, if a cycle is detected then the transaction is aborted. SGT has the theoretically optimal property of avoiding unnecessary aborts, accepting all conflict serializable executions. Despite its advantageous theoretical properties, SGT has seldom been utilized in practical systems owing to the computational costs of maintaining an acyclic graph, notably the cost of cycle checking. Recent work has refuted this perceived wisdom. In [4] it was demonstrated how SGT can be implemented efficiently in a many-core database, offering comparable, and often higher, performance when compared to traditional and contemporary concurrency control protocols.

Despite recent advances, serializable transaction processing performance often remains unsatisfactory for application demands. Another tool at DBMSs disposal to increase performance is to execute transactions at *weak isolation* levels, e.g., Read Committed. Here, the number of permissible schedules is increased at the expense of potentially allowing non-serializable behavior, e.g., *Fuzzy Reads*. Weak isolation is pervasive in real world systems, with most systems offering a range of isolation levels; a comprehensive survey of the isolation levels supported by commercial and open source databases is given in Table 1. A database that allows concurrent transactions to be executed at different isolation levels is said to be *mixed* [5]. For example, transaction $T_{RC}$ can run at Read Committed and transaction $T_S$ at Serializable.

The classical method to implement a mixed DBMS is to opt for a 2PL-variant in which transactions to vary the duration they hold locks [6]. For example, $T_{RC}$ would release read locks on data items immediately after performing the read operation, whereas $T_S$ holds all locks until commit time. This mechanism and others used in mixed DBMSs suffer from the same problem as their serializable equivalents: some valid executions are prevented leading to unnecessary aborts. This begs the question, how can SGT be extended to support transactions executed at weak isolation levels, whilst accepting all and only valid executions? Such an approach would permit higher concurrency and performance. In [5] Adya provides a graph-based system model for defining weak isolation and describes the *mixing-correct theorem*, a correctness criteria for a mixed schedule. This paper presents *mixed serialization graph testing* (MSGT), which accept all valid schedules under the mixing-correct theorem, thus maintaining SGT's property of minimizing aborts. We evaluate MSGT's performance using the YCSB benchmark [7] that has been adapted to generate transactions with different isolation requirements.

The rest of the paper is structured as follows: Sect. 2 provides an overview of serialization graph testing and discusses the adaptations made in [4] to optimize SGT for a many-core DBMS. Section 3 provides a survey of isolation levels supported by 24 DBMSs highlighting the prevalence of mixed DBMSs and demonstrating the utility of MSGT. Section 4 describes Adya's mixing-correct theorem. Section 5 presents mixed serialization graph testing. Section 6 evaluates MSGT using the YCSB benchmark, before Sect. 7 concludes.

## 2    Serialization Graph Testing

This section presents serialization graph testing. Section 2.1 describes the conflict graph theorem and how it is used by SGT. In Sect. 2.2, the algorithmic adjustments made in [4] are given, before Sect. 2.3 describes the many-core optimized graph data structure used in [4], which serves as the basis for mixed serialization graph testing.

### 2.1    Protocol Description

An execution of transactions can be represented by a *schedule*, a time ordered sequence of their operations. For example, consider transactions $T_1$, $T_2$, and $T_3$ shown in schedule $s$ below.

$$s = w_1[x]\ r_2[x]\ r_2[y]\ w_1[y]\ w_2[z]\ w_3[z]\ r_3[x]\ r_3[a]\ w_4[a]\ c_1\ c_3\ c_2\ c_4$$

This schedule can be represented by a *conflict graph* $CG(s)$, shown in Fig. 1. Nodes represent transactions and conflicting operations $a_i$ of $T_i$ and $b_j$ of $T_j$ such that $a_i[x] < b_j[x]$, where $T_i \neq T_j$, are represented by an edge $T_i \rightarrow T_j$; possible conflict pairs are $(a, b) \in [(r, w), (w, r), (w, w)]$. For example, in $s$, $T_2$ reads $x$ after $T_1$ writes to $x$, thus there exists an edge from $T_1$ to $T_2$ in Fig. 1. Changing the order of conflicting operations *could* alter the behavior of at least one transaction. Therefore, an execution of transactions is conflict serializable if a serial ordering of transactions that satisfies all conflict edges can be found. Such a serial ordering exists iff the conflict graph is acyclic. This is known as the *conflict graph theorem* [1]. Note, $s$ is not conflict serializable because $CG(s)$ in Fig. 1 contains a cycle.

**Theorem 1 (Conflict Graph Theorem).** *A schedule $s$ is conflict serializable iff its corresponding conflict graph $CG(s)$ is acyclic.*

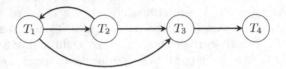

**Fig. 1.** Conflict graph representation of $s$.

SGT directly utilizes the conflict graph theorem by maintaining an acyclic conflict graph. For each operation, conflicts are determined and edges inserted into the graph. An important point to note is the orientation of edge insertions: a transaction only inserts edges incoming to *itself*. After edge insertion, a cycle check is performed *before* executing the operation. If executing the operation would introduce a cycle the offending transaction is aborted and its edges removed. At commit time, a final cycle check is executed, if no cycle is found the transaction commits and removes its edges. In short, SGT provides serializability by ensuring the acyclic invariant.

## 2.2 Algorithmic Adjustments

Due to space constraints nodes must be pruned from the conflict graph. The SGT algorithm sketched in Sect. 2.1 allows transactions to commit with incoming edges if they pass a cycle check. Under this scheme simply deleting nodes of committed transactions can lead to subtle serialization violations. Assume in Fig. 1, $T_3$ has committed and $T_2$ is active. If $T_3$ is removed upon commitment, $T_2$ may subsequently perform an operation that introduces a cycle with $T_3$, but which goes undetected due to $T_3$'s removal, introducing a serialization error. To solve this, in [4] a transaction can commit iff it has no incoming edges, else delaying until this condition is met. As transactions only insert edges incoming to themselves, after issuing a commit request, no more incoming edges are added. Thus, once all incoming edges are removed from the committing node, via the parent node aborting or committing, it will not be in a cycle.

This rule also achieves two desirable properties: *recoverability* and *order preservation*. Recoverability ensures failures do not leave the database in an inconsistent state. In $s$, $T_1$ writes $x$, then $T_2$ reads $x$. If $T_2$ commits before $T_1$, $T_1$ may subsequently abort, at which point $T_2$ has read from a value that never existed. Delaying $T_2$'s commit until it has no incoming edges prevents this issue; if $T_1$ aborts then $T_2$ is also aborted. *Order preservation* ensures the real-time commit order matches the serialization order. In $s$, $T_4$ overwrites the value $a$ read by $T_3$, thus in the serial order: $T_3 \rightarrow T_4$. If $T_4$ commits before $T_3$ no recoverability issues are introduced, but the real-time commit order does not match the serialization order. Delaying $T_4$'s commit until it has no incoming edges avoids this, providing users with an improved, more intuitive, experience.

## 2.3 Many-Core Optimizations

Many-core DBMSs use optimistic approaches as their pessimistic counterparts suffer from poor performance as the core count increases. A common bottleneck in optimistic approaches is an exclusive single-threaded verification phase. Regards SGT, in [4] to avoid a global lock for graph operations, a data structure with a node-local locking protocol is used. Nodes in the graph each store a transaction status (committed, active, aborted) and two sets of pointers representing incoming and outgoing edges. Nodes can then be locked in two modes:

- ***Shared mode:*** transactions can concurrently access the node for edge insertions, edge deletions, and cycle checking. Edge sets guarantee thread-safe concurrent access for scans, insertions, and deletes under the shared lock.
- ***Exclusive mode:*** used for the commit-critical check for incoming edges.

The protocol works as follows: when a transaction $T_x$ identifies a conflict with transaction $T_y$ it first checks if an edge already exists from $T_y$ to $T_x$, if so, no additional work is needed. Else, $T_x$ acquires a shared lock on $T_y$'s node. If $T_y$ is active, then an edge pointer to $T_x$ is inserted into $T_y$'s outgoing edge set and an edge pointer from $T_y$ is inserted into $T_x$'s incoming edge set. $T_x$ then checks for a cycle using a *reduced depth-first search* (DFS) algorithm. Reduced DFS begins at the validating node ($T_x$) and traverses only the portion of the graph that is needed; each step holds nodes in shared lock mode. At commit time, $T_x$ acquires an exclusive lock on its node and checks for incoming edges. If there are none, $T_x$ commits and shared locks are acquired on each node in $T_x$'s outgoing edge set and the edge from $T_x$ removed. Else, there exists at least one incoming edge and the exclusive lock is released and the check is repeated. Another common bottleneck is the reliance on a global timestamp allocator, this is avoided in [4] by letting conflict graph nodes double up as transaction ids.

SGT requires a mechanism to derive conflicts. In [4] rows store a sequential history of accesses. Each access stores the operation type, read or write, and the transaction id. Decoupling the access information from the graph data structure decreases contention. Note, sequentially ordered access is ensured by per-row spin-locks which are released immediately after the operation completes, i.e., the lock is not held until commit time, an improvement over lock-based approaches.

In summary, the SGT implementation in [4] uses a commit rule to simplify node removal, decouples conflict detection, and employs a highly parallel graph structure that allows concurrent cycle checking. In particular, this protocol scales well as the commit critical check only shortly blocks other threads from accessing a node and only the part of the conflict graph needed for validation is traversed. Lastly, it minimizes unnecessary aborts, accepting all conflict serializable schedules and provides an ideal baseline for the development of MSGT.

## 3  Mixing in the Wild

This section motivates the development of a mixed graph-based scheduler that minimizes unneccessary aborts by surveying the isolation levels supported by commercial and open source DBMSs.

It is rare for practical DBMSs to offer applications only a singular isolation level, instead permitting transactions to be run at different isolation levels. In order to assess this claim we surveyed the isolation levels offered by 24 DBMSs in Table 1[1]. Classification was performed based on each database's public documentation. We found 7 isolation levels represented: Read Uncommitted, Read Committed, Cursor Stability, Snapshot Isolation, Consistent Read, Repeatable Read, and Serializable. Note, the exact behavior of each isolation level is highly system-dependent. Interestingly, we found 18 databases supported multiple isolation levels. Of systems offering a singular isolation level Serializable was the most common; these systems were typically NewSQL [8] systems, e.g., CockroachDB [9]. This may suggest a trend away from mixed DBMSs, however, TiDB recently added support for Consistent Read isolation [10] indicating the utility of weaker isolation in practical systems remains.

## 4  Mixing Theory

This section presents the correctness criteria utilized by MSGT. Section 4.1 reproduces the system model from [5], which is used to define weak isolation levels in Sect. 4.2, before the mixing-correct theorem is defined in Sect. 4.3.

### 4.1  System Model

In Adya's system model, transactions consist of an ordered sequence of read and write operations to an arbitrary set of data items, book-ended by a BEGIN operation and a COMMIT or an ABORT operation. The set of items a transaction reads from and writes to is termed its *item read set* and *item write set*. Each write creates a *version* of an item, which is assigned a unique timestamp taken from a totally ordered set (e.g., natural numbers) version $i$ of item $x$ is denoted $x_i$; hence, a multiversioned system is assumed. All data items have an initial *unborn* version $\perp$ produced by an initial transaction $T_{\perp}$. The unborn version is located at the start of each item's version order. An execution of transactions

---

[1]  * Indicates the default setting, [a] Referred to as Read Stability, [b] Behaves like Read Committed due to MVCC implementation, [c] Implemented as Snapshot Isolation, [d] Requires manual lock management, [e] Behaves like Consistent Read.

**Table 1.** Isolation Levels Supported by Open Source & Commercial DBMSs.

| Database System | Isolation Level | | | | | | |
|---|---|---|---|---|---|---|---|
| | RU | RC | CS | SI | CR | RR | S |
| Actian Ingres 11.0 | ✓ | ✓ | ✓ | ✗ | ✗ | ✓ | ✓* |
| Clustrix 5.2 | ✗ | ✓^e | ✗ | ✗ | ✗ | ✓*c | ✓ |
| CockroachDB 20.1.5 | ✗ | ✗ | ✗ | ✗ | ✗ | ✗ | ✓* |
| Google Spanner | ✗ | ✗ | ✗ | ✗ | ✗ | ✗ | ✓* |
| Greenplum 6.8 | ✓^b | ✓* | ✗ | ✗ | ✗ | ✓ | ✗ |
| Dgraph 20.07 | ✗ | ✗ | ✗ | ✓* | ✗ | ✗ | ✗ |
| FaunaDB 2.12 | ✗ | ✗ | ✗ | ✓ | ✗ | ✗ | ✓* |
| Hyper | ✗ | ✗ | ✗ | ✗ | ✗ | ✗ | ✓ |
| IBM Db2 for z/OS 12.0 | ✓ | ✓^a | ✓* | ✗ | ✗ | ✓ | ✗ |
| MySQL 8.0 | ✓ | ✓ | ✗ | ✗ | ✗ | ✓* | ✓ |
| MemGraph 1.0 | ✗ | ✗ | ✗ | ✓* | ✗ | ✗ | ✗ |
| MemSQL 7.1 | ✗ | ✓*e | ✗ | ✗ | ✗ | ✗ | ✗ |
| MS SQL Server 2019 | ✓ | ✓* | ✗ | ✓ | ✗ | ✓ | ✓ |
| Neo4j 4.1 | ✗ | ✓* | ✗ | ✗ | ✗ | ✗ | ✓ |
| NuoDB 4.1 | ✗ | ✓ | ✗ | ✗ | ✓* | ✗ | ✗ |
| Oracle 11g 11.2 | ✗ | ✓* | ✗ | ✓ | ✗ | ✗ | ✗ |
| Oracle BerkeleyDB | ✓ | ✓ | ✓ | ✓ | ✗ | ✗ | ✓ |
| Oracle BerkeleyDB JE | ✓ | ✓ | ✗ | ✗ | ✗ | ✓* | ✓ |
| Postgres 12.4 | ✓^b | ✓* | ✗ | ✗ | ✗ | ✓^c | ✓ |
| SAP HANA | ✗ | ✓* | ✗ | ✓ | ✗ | ✗ | ✗ |
| SQLite 3.33 | ✓ | ✗ | ✗ | ✗ | ✗ | ✗ | ✓* |
| TiDB 4.0 | ✗ | ✗ | ✗ | ✓* | ✓ | ✗ | ✗ |
| VoltDB 10.0 | ✗ | ✗ | ✗ | ✗ | ✗ | ✗ | ✓* |
| YugaByteDB 2.2.2 | ✗ | ✗ | ✗ | ✓* | ✗ | ✗ | ✓ |

on a database is represented by a *history*, $H$. This consists of a *partial order of events*, which reflects (i) each transaction's read and write operations, (ii) data item versions read and written and (iii) commit or abort operations, and a *version order*, which imposes a total order on committed data item versions.

There are three types of dependencies between transactions, which capture the ways in which transactions can *directly* conflict. *Read dependencies* capture the scenario where a transaction reads another transaction's write. *Antidependencies* capture the scenario where a transaction overwrites the version another transaction reads. *Write dependencies* capture the scenario where a transaction overwrites the version another transaction writes. Their definitions are as follows:

**Read-Depends.** Transaction $T_j$ directly *read-depends* (wr) on $T_i$ if $T_i$ writes some version $x_k$ and $T_j$ reads $x_k$.

**Anti-Depends.** Transaction $T_j$ directly *anti-depends* (rw) on $T_i$ if $T_i$ reads some version $x_k$ and $T_j$ writes $x$'s next version after $x_k$ in the version order.

**Write-Depends.** Transaction $T_j$ directly *write-depends* (ww) on $T_i$ if $T_i$ writes some version $x_k$ and $T_j$ writes $x$'s next version after $x_k$ in the version order.

Using these definitions, a history can be represented by a *direct serialization graph*, $DSG(H)$. Nodes correspond to committed transactions and edges mark *direct dependencies*, or conflicts, between transactions. Again the direction of these dependencies indicate the apparent order of transactions in a serial execution. Anomalies are defined by stating properties about the $DSG$.

To illustrate the difference between an Adya history and a schedule, $s$ from Sect. 2 is given again with versions accessed by each operation (version order: $[x_0 \ll x_1, y_0 \ll y_1, z_2 \ll z_3, a_0 \ll a_4]$). Figure 2 shows $DSG(H)$.

$$H = w_1[x_1]\ r_2[x_1]\ r_2[y_0]\ w_1[y_1]\ w_2[z_2]\ w_3[z_3]\ r_3[x_1]\ r_3[a_0]\ w_4[a_4]\ c_1\ c_3\ c_2\ c_4$$

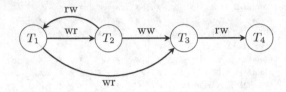

**Fig. 2.** Direct serialization graph representation of $H$.

The above *item-based* model can be extended to handle *predicate-based* operations [5]. Database operations are frequently performed on set of items provided a certain condition called the *predicate*, $P$ holds. When a transaction executes a read or write based on a predicate $P$, the database selects a version for each item to which $P$ applies, this is called the version set of the predicate-based denoted as $Vset(P)$. A transaction $T_j$ changes the matches of a predicate-based read $r_i(P_i)$ if $T_i$ overwrites a version in $Vset(P_i)$.

## 4.2   Weak Isolation Levels

Using the system model in Sect. 4.1, definitions of isolation levels are given via a combination of constraints and the prevention of types of cycles in the $DSG$. In total 11 isolation levels are presented in [5]. To simplify discussions we consider a subset:

- Read Uncommitted: proscribes anomaly *Dirty Write (G0)*, the $DSG$ cannot contain cycles consisting entirely of write-depends edges.
- Read Committed: proscribes *G0* and anomalies, (i) *Aborted Read (G1a)*, transactions cannot read data item versions created by aborted transactions, (ii) *Intermediate Reads (G1b)*, transactions cannot read intermediate data item versions, and (iii) *Circular Information Flow (G1c)*, the $DSG$ cannot contain cycles consisting of write-depends and read-depends edges.
- Repeatable Read: proscribes *G0*, *G1*, and *Write Skew (G2-item)*, the $DSG$ cannot contain cycles containing one or more item-anti-depends edges.
- Serializable: proscribes anomalies *G0*, *G1*, and *G2*, the $DSG$ cannot contain any cycles; this extends the coverage to predicate-anti-depends edges.

## 4.3   Mixing of Isolation Levels

To define a correctness criteria for a mixed DBMS, a $DSG$ variant is used to represent a mixed history, referred to as a *mixed serialization graph*, $MSG(H)$.

A *MSG* only includes *relevant* and *obligatory* conflicts. A relevant conflict is a conflict that is pertinent to a given isolation level, e.g., read-depends edges are relevant to Read Committed transactions but not Read Uncommitted transactions. An obligatory conflict is a conflict that is relevant to one transaction but not the other, e.g., an item-anti-depends edge between a Read Committed transaction and a Serializable transaction is relevant to the Serializable transaction and not the Read Committed transaction but still must be included in the *MSG*. Adya defines the edge inclusion rules for an *MSG* as follows:

1. Write-depends edges are relevant to all transactions regardless of isolation level thus always included.
2. Read-depends edges are relevant for edges incoming to Read Committed, Repeatable Read, or Serializable transactions.
3. Item-anti-depends edges are included for outgoing edges from Repeatable Read and Serializable transactions.
4. Predicate-anti-depends edges are included for outgoing edges from Serializable transactions.

Now in a mixed DBMS, a history is correct if each transaction is provided the isolation guarantees that pertain to its level leading to the *mixing-correct theorem* [5]. Figure 3 illustrates the differences between DSG and MSG representations of a history with the non-relevant and non-obligatory edges removed.

**Theorem 2 (Mixing-Correct Theorem).** *A history H is mixing-correct if* $MSG(H)$ *is acyclic and phenomena G1a and G1b do not occur for Read Committed, Repeatable Read, and Serializable transactions.*

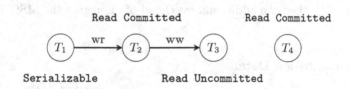

**Fig. 3.** Mixed serialization graph representation of $H$.

# 5   Mixed Serialization Graph Testing

This section presents mixed serialization graph testing. Section 5.1 describes the protocol design. Section 5.2 outlines MSGT's advantages and disadvantages. Lastly, Sect. 5.3 gives implementation details.

## 5.1   Protocol Design

MSGT blends together the SGT implementation from Sect. 2 with the mixing-correct theorem from Sect. 4. Rather than using the graph data structure in Sect. 2.3 to represent a conflict graph, in MSGT it is used to represent a mixed serialization graph with one addition: nodes include transaction's desired isolation level. For each operation, conflicts are determined using the transaction's isolation level and the edge inclusion rules for a mixed serialization graph enumerated in Sect. 4.3: when a transaction $T_i$ detects a conflict with $T_j$ it is inserted into the mixed graph if the conflict is relevant to $T_i$ or obligatory for $T_j$. No changes are necessary to the per-row meta-data as all direct dependencies can be derived from the access history. After edge insertion, a cycle check is performed *before* executing the operation. If executing the operation would introduce a cycle the offending transaction is aborted. At commit time, as in [4] a transaction can commit if and only if it has no incoming edges. This simplifies node deletion and provides order preservation. Note, recoverability in no longer ensured as under the mixing-correct theorem it is permissible for a Read Uncommitted transaction to read from a transaction that subsequently aborts.

## 5.2   Discussion

As seen in Sect. 3 many DBMSs offer weak isolation levels and thus a considerable portion of applications are built atop such guarantees. Typically, mixed isolation is an after thought as DBMSs chase performance, in MSGT mixed isolation is a catered for as a *first-class citizen*. Such an approach provides a higher degree of concurrency and hence performance, whilst also providing the optimal property of no unnecessary aborts.

It is worth noting the utility of weak isolation is limited to applications that can tolerate potentially non-serializable behavior. Additionally, if a workload exhibits low contention or is designed in a manner such that anomalies provably do not occur [11], then the additional overhead of managing the MSG has little benefit.

## 5.3   Implementation Details

MSGT was implemented in our prototype in-memory DBMS which has a plug-gable concurrency control module[2]. The DBMS has a pool of worker threads and each transaction is pinned to a specific worker thread for its duration. Each worker thread has an independent workload generator. Thus when a transaction is committing we repeatedly execute the commit routine (check for incoming edges).

To ensure high operation throughput under a concurrent workload data structures use atomic operations were appropriate. For safe memory reclamation in a concurrent environment epoch-based garbage collection is used [12] and nodes' edge sets are recycled after a transaction is committed and deleted.

Adya's system model is defined in terms of a multiversion model, but as the MSGT scheduler allows transactions to optimistically read dirty records, the possibility of cascading aborts is introduced. Unwinding writes due to cascading

---

[2] https://github.com/jackwaudby/spaghetti.

aborts lead to unnecessary system load and which is not useful for both user and system. Therefore, only one uncommitted transaction is allowed to modify a data item. Also, the prototype DBMS does not currently support predicate-based operations, thus an item-based read/write model is assumed. Hence, some isolation levels, e.g., Repeatable Read can not be captured.

## 6  Evaluation

In this section, we experimentally compare MSGT with SGT using our prototype in-memory DBMS. The evaluation focuses on two implementations: a graph-based scheduler (SGT) and a mixed graph-based scheduler (MSGT).

Experiments were performed using an Azure Standard D48v3 instance with 48 virtualized CPU cores and 192 GB of memory. Prior to each experiment, tables are loaded, followed by a warm-up period, before a measurement period; both are of configurable length, we use 60 s and 5 min respectively. We measure the following metrics:

- **Throughput:** number of transactions committed per second.
- **Abort rate:** rate at which transactions are being aborted.
- **Average latency:** the latency time of committed transactions (in $ms$) averaged across the measurement period.

Our experiments use the Yahoo! Cloud Serving Benchmark (YCSB) [7]. YCSB was originally designed to evaluate large-scale Internet applications, it is re-purposed here as a microbenchmark to allow various aspects of an OLTP workload to be altered. Specifically, we tweak the proportion of serializable transactions, differ the contention level, and increase the core count to measure scalability. YCSB has a one table with a primary key and 10 additional columns each with 100B of random characters. For all our experiments, we use a YCSB table of 100K rows. There are two types of transaction: read or update, each contains 10 independent operations accessing 10 distinct items. Update transactions consist of 5 reads and 5 writes that occur in random order. Read transactions consist solely of read operations. The proportion of update transactions is controlled by the parameter, $U$, it is fixed to 50% for our experiments. Data access follows a Zipfian distribution, where the frequency of access to hot records is tuned using a skew parameter, $\theta$. When $\theta = 0$, data is accessed with uniform frequency, and when $\theta = 0.9$ it is extremely skewed. In order to measure the impact of transactions running at weaker isolation we introduce an additional parameter, $\omega$, which controls the proportion of transactions running at Serializable isolation. The remainder are split between Read Committed (90%) and Read Uncommitted (10%).

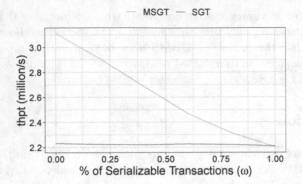

**Fig. 4.** Throughput as serializable transactions ($\omega$) varied from 0% to 100%.

## 6.1 Isolation

We begin with measuring the impact of increasing the proportion of transactions executing at Serializable isolation from 0% to 100%. This aims to test MSGT's ability to leverage its theoretical properties to offer increased performance when transactions are run at weaker isolation levels. For this experiment, we opt for a medium contention level, $\theta = 0.8$, and the framework is configured to run with 40 cores.

In Fig. 4, SGT's throughput is invariant to the proportion of Serializable transactions, this is anticipated as it is unable to take advantage of transactions' declared isolation levels, in effect, executing all transactions at Serializable. Meanwhile, the throughput of MSGT decreases as $\omega$ is increased, converging towards SGT's throughput. When there are no Serializable transactions ($\omega = 0.0$), MSGT achieves a 39% increase in throughput. At $\omega = 0.4$, this drops to a 21% increase and at $\omega = 0.8$ a 4% gain is exhibited. When $\omega = 1.0$, SGT marginally outperforms MSGT, this can be attributed to the additional overhead of managing the MSG. This relationship is reflected in the abort rate displayed in Fig. 5a, across the range of $\omega$, SGT's abort rate varies from a 3x increase over MSGT's abort rate to an equivalent abort rate when all transactions are executed at Serializable. A higher abort rate degrades the user experience, reduces throughput and, as can be seen in Fig. 5b, harms latency.

## 6.2 Contention

In the next experiment we measure the effect of increasing contention in the system by varying $\theta$ from 0.6 to 0.9. Contention happens when multiple transactions try to read or write the same database item. In theory, contention increases the chance of conflicts between transactions. This should translate into an increase in the number of edges inserted into the conflict graph. Under SGT all edges are inserted, whereas, MSGT utilizes isolation levels to be more selective over edge insertions (only adding relevant or obligatory edges) hence it inserts less

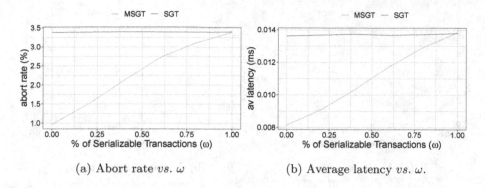

(a) Abort rate *vs.* $\omega$          (b) Average latency *vs.* $\omega$.

**Fig. 5.** Serializable transactions ($\omega$) varied from 0% to 100%.

edges into the conflict graph, and should find less cycles (aborts) compared to SGT. We set the proportion of Serializable transactions to $\omega = 0.2$. Again the experiment was run with 40 cores.

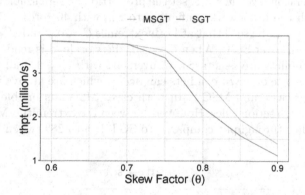

**Fig. 6.** Throughput as contention factor ($\theta$) varied from 0.6 to 0.9.

Figure 6 displays the throughput of SGT and MSGT as the contention is increased. As $\theta$ increases the throughput decreases for both protocols. For low levels of contention SGT performs marginally better than MSGT (<1% difference), but under high contention this reverses and MSGT offers a 24% increase in throughput. Figure 7a shows that after $\theta = 0.7$, the abort rate begins increasing for both protocols. At the highest level of contention ($\theta = 0.9$), 0.1% of the data is accessed by 35% of the queries, and SGT aborts 17% more transactions than MSGT. Lastly, in Fig. 7b, above $\theta = 0.7$, MSGT achieves between a 9% and 28% reduction in the average latency.

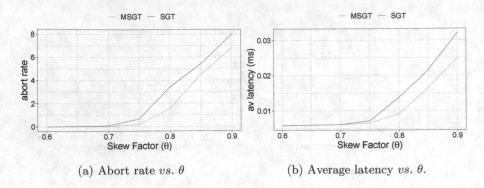

(a) Abort rate *vs.* $\theta$                    (b) Average latency *vs.* $\theta$.

**Fig. 7.** Contention factor ($\theta$) varied from 0.6 to 0.9.

## 6.3   Update Rate

For the next experiment, we explore the effect of varying the proportion of update operations ($U$) within each transaction. For this experiment, we opt for a medium contention level, $\theta = 0.8$, set the proportion of Serializable transactions to $\omega = 0.2$, with the framework configured to run with 40 cores.

From Fig. 8 it can be seen that at both extremes $U = 0.0$ and $U = 1.0$ MSGT displays no benefit over SGT. When $U = 0.0$, the workload is read-only thus no (ww, wr, rw) conflicts are generated. Conversely, with $U = 1.0$ all transactions are write-only, hence only ww conflicts can occur, which are always inserted into the graph under SGT and MSGT. In both cases MSGT is unable leverage its selective conflict detection rules. However, between the extremities MSGT is able to produce higher throughput compared to SGT (up to 28% when $U = 0.2$).

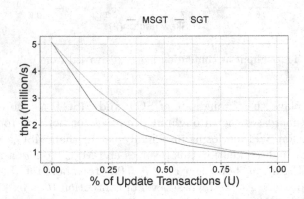

**Fig. 8.** Throughput as update rate transactions ($U$) varied from 0.0 to 1.0.

## 6.4   Scalability

In this experiment we fix the workload factors and vary the core count (1 to 40) to evaluate MSGT's scalability compared to SGT. We anticipate that MSGT scales better than SGT as its scheduler generally performs less work (edge insertions and cycle checking). From Fig. 9a it can be seen that until 20 cores the throughput of both protocols is indistinguishable; in fact, up to 10 cores SGT exhibits between a 1.2% and 3.1% increase over MSGT. After this point, a gap appears, at 30 cores MSGT has 13.1% higher throughput and at 40 cores this difference increases to 27.9%.

In Fig. 9b it can be seen the abort rate of the protocols starts to diverge after 10 cores: SGT has an abort rate of 1.65% and 3.39% at 30 and 40 cores respectively, whereas, MSGT's is 0.50% and 1.54%.

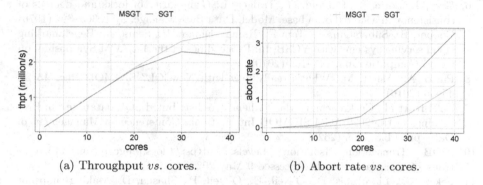

(a) Throughput *vs.* cores.          (b) Abort rate *vs.* cores.

**Fig. 9.** Core count varied 1 to 40.

## 7   Conclusion

In this paper we presented mixed serialization graph testing, a graph-based scheduler that leverages Adya's mixing-correct theorem to permit transactions to execute at different isolation levels. When workloads contain transactions running at weaker isolation levels, MSGT is able to outperform serializable graph-based concurrency control by up to 28%. Additionally, MSGT scales as the number of cores is increased, an important property given modern hardware. Like SGT, MSGT minimizes the number of aborted transactions, accepting all useful schedules under the mixing-correct theorem, which greatly improves user experience. As part of future work we wish to extend our performance evaluation to include industry standard benchmarks such as TPCx-IoT [13] and TPC-C [14]. In summary, this paper strengthens recent work refuting the assumption that graph-based concurrency control is impractical.

**Acknowledgements.** J. Waudby was supported by the Engineering and Physical Sciences Research Council, Centre for Doctoral Training in Cloud Computing for Big Data [grant number EP/L015358/1].

# References

1. Bernstein, P., Hadzilacos, V., Goodman, N.: Concurrency control and recovery in database systems (1987)
2. Eswaran, K., Gray, J., Lorie, R., Traiger, I.: The notions of consistency and predicate locks in a database system. Commun. ACM **19**(11), 624–63 (1976)
3. Kung, H., Robinson, J.: On optimistic methods for concurrency control. ACM Trans. Database Syst. **6**(2), 213–226 (1981)
4. Durner, D., Neumann, T.: No false negatives: accepting all useful schedules in a fast serializable many-core system. In: 35th IEEE International Conference on Data Engineering, pp. 734–745 (2019)
5. Adya, A.: Weak Consistency: A Generalized Theory and Optimistic Implementations for Distributed Transactions. PhD Thesis, Massachusetts Institute of Technology (1999)
6. Gray, J., Lorie, R., Putzolu, G., Traiger, I.: Granularity of locks and degrees of consistency in a shared data base. Model. Data Base Manage. Syst. 365–394 (1976)
7. Cooper, B., Silberstein, A., Tam E., Ramakrishnan, R., Sears, R.: Benchmarking cloud serving systems with YCSB. In: Proceedings of the 1st ACM Symposium on Cloud Computing, pp. 143–154 (2010)
8. Pavlo, A., Aslett, M.: What's really new with NewSQL? SIGMOD Rec. **45**(2), 45–55 (2016)
9. Taft, R. et al.: CockroachDB: the resilient geo-distributed SQL database. In: Proceedings of the 2020 ACM SIGMOD International Conference on Management of Data, pp. 1493–1509 (2020)
10. TiDB Transaction Isolation Levels. https://docs.pingcap.com/tidb/dev/transaction-isolation-levels. Accessed 9 May 2022
11. Fekete, A., Liarokapis, D., O'Neil, E., O'Neil, P., Shasha, D.: Making snapshot isolation serializable. ACM Trans. Database Syst. **30**(2), 492–528 (2005)
12. Fraser, K.: Practical lock-freedom. PhD Thesis, University of Cambridge (2004)
13. Poess, M., Nambiar, R., Kulkarni, K., Narasimhadevara, C., Rabl, T., Jacobsen, H.A.: Analysis of TPCx-IoT: the first industry standard benchmark for IoT gateway systems. In: 34th IEEE International Conference on Data Engineering, pp. 1519–1530 (2018)
14. TPC Benchmark C, revision 5.11. www.tpc.org/tpc_documents_current_versions/pdf/tpc-c_v5.11.0.pdf. Accessed 19 July 2022

# BoDS: A Benchmark on Data Sortedness

Aneesh Raman[1(✉)], Konstantinos Karatsenidis[1], Subhadeep Sarkar[1],
Matthaios Olma[2], and Manos Athanassoulis[1]

[1] Boston University, Boston, MA, USA
{aneeshr,karatse,ssarkar1,mathan}@bu.edu
[2] Microsoft Research, Redmond, WA, USA
maolma@microsoft.com

**Abstract.** Indexes in data systems accelerate data access by adding
structure to otherwise unstructured data at the cost of index construction and maintenance. Data systems, and particularly, the underlying
indexing data structures are designed to offer favorable ingestion (and
query) performance for the two extremes of data sortedness, i.e., *unsorted*
data (often assumed to follow a uniform random distribution) or *fully-
sorted* data. However, in practice, data may arrive with an intermediate
degree of pre-sortedness. In such cases, where data arrives nearly (but not
necessarily fully) sorted, the intuition is that the indexing cost should be
lower than when ingesting unsorted data. Such sortedness-aware index
designs lack from the literature. In fact, there is a need for a framework
to explore how index designs may be able to exploit pre-existing sortedness during data ingestion to amortize the index construction cost.

In this paper, we present *Benchmark on Data Sortedness, BoDS* for
short, that highlights the performance of data systems in terms of index
construction and navigation costs when operating on data ingested with
variable sortedness. To quantify *data sortedness*, we use the state-of-the-
art $(K, L)$-sortedness metric. Specifically, BoDS benchmarks the indexing
performance of a data system as we vary the two fundamental components of the metric: (i) $K$, that measures *how many* elements are out-
of-order in a data collection; and (ii) $L$, that measures by *how much* the
out-of-order entries are displaced from their respective in-order positions;
as well as (iii) the distribution of $L$. We present in detail the benchmark,
and we run it on PostgreSQL, a popular, production-grade relational
database system. Unsurprisingly, we observe that PostgreSQL cannot
exploit data sortedness; however, through our experiments we show the
headroom for improvement, and we lay the groundwork for experimentation with sortedness-aware index designs. The code for BoDS is available
at: https://github.com/BU-DiSC/bods.

**Keywords:** Sortedness · Indexing · Databases

## 1 Introduction

To facilitate efficient query processing, database systems often utilize indexes
that are gradually populated as new data is ingested [3,4,6,9,10,18]. Indexes

R. Nambiar and M. Poess (Eds.): TPCTC 2022, LNCS 13860, pp. 17–32, 2023.
https://doi.org/10.1007/978-3-031-29576-8_2

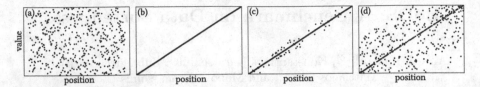

**Fig. 1.** Classical data organization techniques like indexing in databases focus on the two extremes of data sortedness, i.e., (a) scrambled data, and (b) fully-sorted data. However, there is a lack of a clear framework to evaluate the indexing performance of systems with intermediary degrees of data sortedness as shown in (c) and (d), where data is ordered to some extent.

accelerate data access for both analytical and transactional workloads by efficiently supporting selective queries. They improve query performance by adding structure to an otherwise unstructured data collection at the expense of index construction and maintenance.

**Data Sortedness.** The goal of a range index is to create a fully sorted version of the ingested data (on the indexed attribute). In practice, in several real-life use cases, data arrives with some pre-existing structure, i.e., data may be *near-sorted*, but not necessarily fully sorted on the indexing attribute. For example, in a typical data warehousing benchmark like TPC-H [19], one of the main tables (`lineitem`) has three date columns (`shipdate`, `commitdate`, and `receiptdate`), and when data arrives as ordered on the `shipdate`, the other two date columns on `commitdate` and `receiptdate` are also very close to being sorted (but not fully-sorted) [3]. Near sortedness can also be found in time-series, stock market data, and monitoring measurements that are part of complex hybrid transactional/analytical pipelines. Further, near-sorted data collections often result from a previous query or join operation or sorting based on another naturally correlated attribute [5]. We also have to index near-sorted data when a relation is already sorted based on a collection of attributes, and the index built is a superset of the ranking attributes. In addition to classifying data as *fully sorted* or *not sorted*, there is a wealth of intermediate states of data sortedness. These are captured by *sortedness metrics* [5,8,12,14] which create a continuum between the two extremes. To populate this continuum, we use $(K, L)$-sortedness [5] that allows us to vary *how many* entries are out-of-order and by *how much*.

**Problem: Lack of Sortedness Benchmark for Indexes.** When ingesting data in a heap file, we only need to append it at the end of the file. However, when an index is involved, an *additional* index ingestion effort goes to establish a complete order of the ingested data (based on the index attributes) to facilitate future queries. For workloads that arrive with some pre-existing degree of sortedness, one would expect that the intrinsic data sortedness would reduce the extra effort spent to establish total order to the ingested data and speedup index construction. Despite the *natural correlation between data sortedness and index construction cost*, state-of-the-art database indexing techniques are not (*yet*) designed to take advantage of any intermediate degree of sortedness when ingesting near sorted data. Classical index structures (e.g., B$^+$-trees) focus on the two extremes of data sortedness, i.e., *unsorted* data (regular insertions) and *fully sorted* data [2,7] (visualized in Fig. 1a and 1b), but do not consider the case of near-sorted data (Fig. 1c and 1d). While it is intuitive that indexes should be able to perform better with increasing sortedness, as *less* effort is required to establish total order, practical performance evaluations for indexes and data systems are unexplored. In order to bridge this gap, we propose a new benchmarking framework that analyzes the performance of indexes and data systems by varying data sortedness in a continuum - from scrambled (unsorted) data to fully sorted data. Specifically, in this work, we focus on quantifying indexing performance when ingesting data that is nearly sorted on the indexed attribute.

**Contributions.** To this end, we formalize the **Benchmark on Data Sortedness**[1] (BoDS) that varies data sortedness using the $(K, L)$-sortedness metric [5]. As a first step toward constructing the benchmark, we present a variable-sortedness data generator that builds $(K, L)$-sorted data collections using a user-specified distribution for $L$. The benchmark tests five different workload types: (i) pure bulk loading, (ii) one-by-one insertion only, (iii) mixed inserts and queries without pre-loading, (iv) mixed inserts and queries after preloading using bulk loading, and (v) mixed inserts and queries after preloading using one-by-one insertions. For each of the five workload types, a spectrum of different data ingestion orders are generated using the $(K, L)$-sortedness metric and tested to quantify the combined impact of data sortedness and access pattern types. We highlight that BoDS tests both **bulk insertion** and **transactional read-/write mixed workloads** with a **varying degree of (ingestion) sortedness**. As an example, we benchmark PostgreSQL, a state-of-the-art production-grade database system, and present key observations regarding adapting data systems and indexing to be sortedness-aware.

## 2 Data Sortedness Metrics

In order to vary, study, and exploit data sortedness, we first need a way to quantify it. To that end, several metrics have been proposed and used in literature [5,8,12,14]. Some of these include *inversions* that measure the number of pairs in the incorrect order, *runs* that measure the number of contiguous increasing subsequences in the collection, and *exchanges* that quantify the least number of swaps needed to bring the data in order [12]. While these metrics are intuitive to quantify data sortedness, they have certain drawbacks that make them unsuitable to use in a sortedness benchmark for indexing. For example, *inversions* fail to capture global disorder where the data collection contains monotonically increasing sorted sequences, but the sequences are placed out of order; *runs* fail to capture local disorder, where each entry in the data collection can simply be swapped with its adjacent entry to establish total order [14].

$(K, L)$-**Sortedness Metric.** Ben-Moshe *et al.* proposed to quantify data sortedness using a combination of two parameters: $K$, which captures the number of elements that are out of order, and $L$, which captures the maximum displacement

---

[1] BoDS codebase: https://github.com/BU-DiSC/bods.

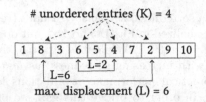

**Fig. 2.** A sample data collection having 10 elements with $K = 4$ and $L = 6$.

in the position of the out-of-order elements [5]. Essentially, the $(K, L)$-sortedness metric captures a data collection's sortedness in terms of *how many elements* $(K)$ are in the *wrong* position, and crucially, *by how much* $(L)$. The combination of both $K$ and $L$ in this metric underlines the *effort* it would take to establish total order in a data collection, while also overriding drawbacks of one-dimensional metrics (discussed above) with respect to global or local disorder. Figure 2 visualizes the $(K, L)$-sortedness metric for a data collection of 10 elements with 4 elements out of order $(K = 4)$ and a maximum displacement of 6 positions $(L = 6)$. The original definition refers to $L$ as maximum displacement, meaning that even if all out-of-order elements are off by one position and only one is off by a higher number, say $max\_disp$, then $L = max\_disp$. When considering files and indexing, one element in a wrong location is not considered detrimental. Hence, we consider one more dimension of near-sortedness in our benchmarking metric: the *distribution of the displacement of the out-of-order entries*.

## 3    Generating $(K, L)$-Sorted Data

The most important part of the proposed benchmark is generating data collections with a varying degree of sortedness. To that end, we build a synthetic data generator that creates data collections adhering to specific values of the $(K, L)$-sortedness metric. The data generator takes as input user-specified values for the $K$ and $L$ parameters of the sortedness metric as a fraction of the total number of entries $(N)$, as well as the displacement distribution (on $L$). The total size of the generated data collection can be controlled using the number of entries to be

**Table 1.** Overview of input arguments to the sortedness data generator.

| Parameter | Description |
|---|---|
| $N$ | No. of entries in the data collection |
| $P$ | Size of the payload for every key |
| $K$ | No. of out-of-order entries in the data collection |
| $L$ | Maximum displacement of an out-of-order entry |
| $B(\alpha, \beta)$ | Beta distribution for displacement (on $L$) |
| $S$ | Seed value |
| $o$ | output directory path |

---

**Algorithm 1:** Generate $(K, L, B)$-sorted keys

---

**Input:** Fully sorted array $arr$, $N \geq 0$; $K \geq 0$; $L \geq 0$; $B(\alpha, \beta)$, $num\_tries1 > 0, num\_tries2 > 0$
**Output:** $(K, L, B)$-sorted array $arr$

```
 1  Sources ← Generate_Sources(N, K) ;                              /* using Algorithm 2 */
 2  dest <>;                                                        /* set of destinations */
 3  left <>;                                                        /* set of left out sources */
 4  for x ∈ Sources do
 5  |    while num_tries1 > 0 do
 6  |    |    r ← Pick_dest(N, K, x, B);                             /* using Algorithm 3 */
 7  |    |    num_tries1 ← num_tries1 − 1;
 8  |    |    if r ∈ dest or r ∈ Sources;                           /* destination already used */
 9  |    |    then
10  |    |    |    if num_tries1 == 0;              /* retrials exhausted, moving r to leftovers */
11  |    |    |    then
12  |    |    |    |    insert r to left;
13  |    |    |    end
14  |    |    |    continue;
15  |    |    else
16  |    |    |    insert r in dest;
17  |    |    |    swap arr[x] with arr[r];
18  |    |    |    break;
19  |    |    end
20  |    end
21  end
22  for x ∈ left;                                             /* randomized re-attempt for leftovers */
23  do
24  |    while num_tries2 > 0 do
25  |    |    r ← Pick_dest(N, K, x, B);                             /* using Algorithm 3 */
26  |    |    num_tries2 ← num_tries2 − 1;
27  |    |    if r ∈ dest or r ∈ Sources;                           /* destination already used */
28  |    |    then
29  |    |    |    continue;
30  |    |    else
31  |    |    |    insert r in dest;
32  |    |    |    swap arr[x] with arr[r];
33  |    |    |    remove x from left;
34  |    |    |    break;
35  |    |    end
36  |    end
37  end
38  Perform_Brute_Force(arr, left, dest, L) ;                       /* using Algorithm 4 */
```

---

generated $(N)$ and the payload size $(P)$. The payload is a randomly generated string of a given size. Table 1 summarizes the input parameters to the workload generator.

**Variable-Sortedness Data Generator.** The data generator initially creates a fully sorted data collection and induces "unsortedness" as required. The overall process is described in detail in Algorithm 1. Unordered entries are generated by swapping elements, i.e., each swap generates two out-of-order elements that contribute to the $K$ parameter. Thus, for a given $K$, the data generator first picks $K/2$ sources for swaps (Algorithm 2), and for each source, a destination position (up to $L$ positions away) is randomly picked to swap with (Algorithm 3).

**Displacement Distribution.** While the $(K, L)$-sortedness metric quantifies the effort required to bring the data collection to fully-sorted order, it does not specify how the unordered entries are distributed within the data collection. The $L$ parameter captures only the maximum displacement among all unordered entries, hence, we may have only one entry that is displaced by $L$, whereas other entries have a much smaller displacement. Thus, to offer fine-grained control on the distribution of the displacement among the unordered entries, we use

**Algorithm 2:** Generate $K/2$ swap sources

**Input:** $N \geq 0; K \geq 0$
**Output:** A set of source swaps $X$
1  $cnt \leftarrow 0$;
2  **while** $cnt < K/2$ **do**
3      pick a random index $r \in [0, n-1]$;
4      **if** $r \in X$ **then**
5          continue;
6      **else**
7          insert $r$ in $X$;
8          $cnt + +$;
9      **end**
10 **end**

**Algorithm 3:** Pick a destination

**Input:** $N \geq 0; K \geq 0$; source $x$; $B(\alpha, \beta)$
**Output:** Destination $d$
1  $low\_jump \leftarrow -L$;
2  $high\_jump \leftarrow L$;
3  **if** $position + high\_jump \geq N$ ;                    /* Sanity checks for out-of-bounds */
4  **then**
5      $high\_jump \leftarrow N - 1 - x$;
6  **end**
7  **if** $position + low\_jump < N$ **then**
8      $low\_jump \leftarrow -x$;
9  **end**
10 pick $r \in [0, 1]$;
11 initialize beta distribution object $distr(B)$;
12 $rd \leftarrow quantile(distr, r)$;                        /* picks number in [0,1] range */
13 $jump \leftarrow low\_jump + ((high\_jump - low\_jump) * rd)$;
14 $ret \leftarrow position + jump$;

**Algorithm 4:** Brute-Force Swap

**Input:** Array $arr$, leftovers $left$, destination swaps $dest$, $L$
**Output:** Array $arr$ after swapping leftovers
1  **for** $x \in left$;                                     /* final brute-force attempt for leftovers */
2  **do**
3      pick $rnd \in [0, 1]$ ;                               /* coin toss for forward/backward run */
4      **if** $rnd < 0.5$;                                   /* move forward */
5      **then**
6          $start \leftarrow x - L; end \leftarrow x + L$;
7      **else**
8          $start \leftarrow x + L; end \leftarrow x - L$;    /* move backward */
9      **end**
10     **for** $r \in [start, end]$;                         /* loop and pick first valid spot */
11     **do**
12         **if** $r \in dest$ or $r == x$ or $r \in X$;     /* check for cascading swaps */
13         **then**
14             continue;
15         **else**
16             insert $r$ in $dest$;
17             swap arr[x] with arr[r];
18             break;
19         **end**
20     **end**
21 **end**

an additional parameter to capture the distribution of data sortedness through a generalized beta distribution with fixed bounds between $-L$ and $L$. Figure 3 shows examples of the probability density (PDF) of the beta distribution. Note that the beta distribution maps to uniform for $\alpha = \beta = 1$ (Fig. 3a) and that it maps to a variable degree of skewed distributions for different values of $\alpha$ and $\beta$ (Fig. 3b, 3c and 3d). Algorithm 3 is already capable of generating swaps with a distance that follows a user-defined distribution (lines 10–14). To do this, we use a generalized beta distribution with user-specified $\alpha$ and $\beta$ values. For this, we use the C++ boost library that provides a beta distribution function and a quantile function for picking a number per the beta distribution using inverse transform sampling.

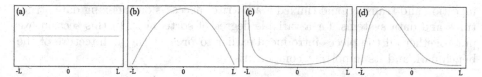

**Fig. 3.** Probability density (PDF) of $\beta$-distribution bounded between $[-L, L]$. Using the $\beta$-distribution offers fine-grained control on the $L$ parameter. In (a) that the displacements are uniformly distributed ($\alpha = \beta = 1$), while in (b) the displacements are centered around the mean $= 0$ ($\alpha = \beta = 2$). Skewness in the distribution of displacements can be introduced like (c) and (d), where they are closer to the maximum displacement ($\alpha = \beta = 0.5$), or biased toward one direction ($\alpha = 2, \beta = 5$).

**Examples of $(K, L)$-Sorted Data.** The data generator is capable of generating data collections with variable $K$, $L$, and displacement distribution. For example, a dataset with either $K = 0\%$ or $L = 0\%$ is fully sorted. Similarly, a dataset with $K = 10\%$ and $L = 2\%$ will have 10% of its total entries out of order, and each out-of-order entry is displaced within a distance equivalent to 2% (at most) of the total entries from its ideal position. Figure 4 shows an example $(K, L, B)$-sorted data collections. Here, we have used $\alpha = \beta = 1$ (uniform distribution) for Fig. 4a–4d, while we use $\alpha = \beta = 0.5$ (skewed) for Fig. 4e–4h. Consequently, we

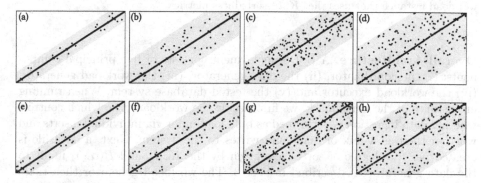

**Fig. 4.** Examples of benchmark data with different $K$ and $L$ combinations for data sortedness. The first row of visuals (a–d) are generated using a uniform distribution ($\alpha = \beta = 1$), while the second row of visuals (e–h) are generated using a skewed distribution concentrated close to the maximum displacement ($\alpha = \beta = 0.5$). The following figures correspond to sortedness levels: for the following sortedness levels: (a)&(e) K = 10%, L = 10%, (b)&(f) K = 20%, L = 25%, (c)&(g) K = 50%, L = 25%, (d)&(h) K = 50%, L = 50%.

observe that a higher number of unordered entries in Fig. 4e–4h are displaced by $\sim L$ as compared to the former set of figures.

## 4    The Benchmark on Data Sortedness

The Benchmark on Data Sortedness is a suite of workloads that compares data ingestion and transactional (mixed read/write) accesses on indexing data structures and data systems, for a variable degree of sortedness. In this section, we put together all the pieces introduced earlier to present the architecture of the benchmark and its important components.

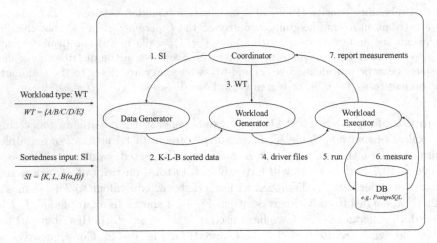

**Fig. 5.** High-level architecture of the proposed Benchmark on Data Sortedness (BoDS) workload instance that uses the $(K, L)$-sortedness metric.

**Overall Architecture.** A BoDS deployment consists of five principal components: (i) the coordinator, (ii) the data generator, (iii) the workload generator, (iv) the workload executor and (v) the tested database system. When running an instance of the benchmark, we first decide the workload type which controls whether data ingestion is performed as bulk loading or via individual inserts and whether there is a mix of reads and writes to the system. Next, a data file is created per the degree of sortedness given by the $K$, $L$, and $B(\alpha, \beta)$ input to the data generator as described in Sect. 3. The workload generator then takes as input the data file and the workload type to generate driver files that prepare the workload according to the system's interface. When testing full-blown relational systems, the system driver files contain SQL statements. A file named `preload.sql` loads the initial data and preconditions the database, and a second file named `operations.sql` contains the interleaved inserts or queries. Finally, the workload executor executes the driver files on the tested system and monitors their runtime. To try variable data sortedness, the workload executor is re-instantiated with different $(K, L)$ inputs. Figure 5 illustrates the high-level architecture of a BoDS workload instance.

**Table 2.** Overview of workloads supported by the Sortedness Benchmark. Workloads A and D use Bulk loading (BL) for the data loading phase, while workloads B and E use Individual inserts (II).

| Workload | Data loading | | Operations | |
|---|---|---|---|---|
| | Method | % of data | R/W ratio | % of data |
| A | BL | 100% | – | – |
| B | II | 100% | – | – |
| C | – | 0% | 17%/83% | 100% |
| D | BL | 80% | 50%/50% | 20% |
| E | II | 80% | 50%/50% | 20% |

**Supported Workloads.** We briefly summarize the workload types in Table 2. Specifically, the benchmark supports five workload types:

(A) bulk load: where we insert data into the system using the bulk load functionality (e.g., copy in PostgreSQL);
(B) individual inserts: where we ingest data into the system one by one;
(C) mixed inserts and read queries with no preloading: where we insert data interleaved with (17%) reads;
(D) mixed inserts and read queries after bulk loading (a combination of A and C): where we pre-load the system with a portion of the data using bulk loading and perform interleaved reads and writes;
(E) mixed inserts and read queries after individual inserts (a combination of B and C): where we pre-load the system with a portion of the data using individual insertions and perform interleaved reads and writes;

For the mixed workloads (D) and (E), we use 80% of the to-be-ingested data to preload the system and perform mixed reads and writes on the remaining data. Also, the lookup keys are uniformly chosen and may consist of both empty and non-empty queries within the key domain. Essentially, workload C model performance during the initialization-state of the index, while workloads D and E capture the steady-state performance.

## 5   BoDS in Action

We run the Benchmark on Data Sortedness (BoDS) on PostgreSQL, a popular row-store and present key observations regarding its performance when ingesting nearly-sorted data.

**Experimental Setup.** We run the experiments on Amazon Web Services (AWS) EC2 instances of t2.medium instance type. Each instance has 2 virtual Intel(R) Xeon(R) CPU E5-2686 v4 @ 2.30 GHz CPUs, 4 GB DIMM RAM and 40 GB root storage using general purpose SSDs (gp2) with 120 provisioned IOPS on EBS storage. The instances run Ubuntu Server 22.04 LTS (HVM) that use a 64-bit (x86) architecture.

**Default System and Index Setup.** We use PostgreSQL 14.3 to execute the benchmark with a modified buffer pool (shared buffer) space of 1 GB. In all experiments, we use *unlogged* tables to avoid overheads due to write-ahead logging (WAL) and isolate index performance. We ingest data in a table containing two attributes: (i) id_col, and (ii) payload. A B-tree is created (before data ingestion/loading) on the id_col attribute. In each experiment, we drop the existing table (if it exists) along with its corresponding index, and recreate them.

**Default Data Setup.** We create multiple data collections (of size 4 GB) with varying $K$ and $L$ values using a uniform distribution ($\alpha = \beta = 1$). Each data collection is created with 16M key-value pairs having an entry size of 256 B, where each key is 4 B and the payload is 252 B.

**Default Testing Suite.** BoDS supports execution of any combination of $(K, L)$ and $B(\alpha, \beta)$ for a particular workload type. By default, we run the benchmark for the following $(K, L)$-near-sorted combinations: $(100, 1)$, $(50, 1)$, $(25, 1)$, $(10, 1)$, $(5, 1)$, $(1, 1)$, $(0, 0)$, $(1, 5)$, $(1, 10)$, $(1, 25)$, $(1, 50)$, $(1, 100)$, and $(100, 100)$. This way, we ensure to compare the systems for a spectrum of near-sortedness, in addition to the two extremes of *fully-sorted* data and *unsorted* data.

**Evaluation Metrics.** We measure using BoDS the performance of PostgreSQL measuring: (i) ingestion latency, and (ii) overall operational latency in case of a mixed workload with reads and writes.

## 5.1  Raw Ingestion Performance

In this set of experiments, we compare the performance of the PostgreSQL (Postgres) system while bulk loading and one-by-one insert into a database table using a B-tree index. For bulk loading, we use the COPY command to load the table with the entire data file. In the case of individual inserts, we write an INSERT command for each row of the data collection. In both cases, the commands are written to the load.sql file, and we measure the overall execution time while executing this file on Postgres. Figure 6 shows the comparison of bulk loading and individual inserts with near-sorted data, using a B-tree index for Postgres.

**Bulk Loading is Extremely Fast.** As expected, we observe from Fig. 6 that bulk loading (black line) in PostgreSQL is extremely fast, with an average ingestion latency of 5.62 $\mu$s per inserted row. This is because bulk loading populates the index bottom-up by first creating fully-occupied leaf and internal nodes of the b-tree index. This allows PostgreSQL to avoid expensive node splits for both leaf and internal nodes as well as re-organizing the data layout. However, bulk

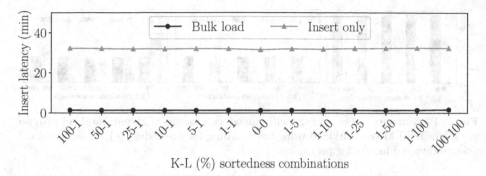

K-L (%) sortedness combinations

**Fig. 6.** Comparison of bulk loading and insert performance of PostgreSQL with near-sorted data of 16M rows (4GiB).

loading the data entails sorting the entire collection up front. This is why ingesting a fully sorted ($K=L=0$) data set (82 s) takes 19.51% less time as compared to ingesting unsorted ($K=L=100$) data (98 s). Note that this improvement in performance is owing only to a smaller sorting overhead before bulk loading.

**PostgreSQL is Agnostic Toward Data Sortedness.** Figure 6 (red line) also shows that when performing individual insertions, PostgreSQL is unable to take advantage of any intermediary data sortedness. The sortedness-agnostic ingestion performance of PostgreSQL can be attributed to the underlying B-tree index, the construction cost of which is $O(log_F N)$ (since there is no bulk loading happening in this case) due to tree-traversal. The B-tree does not use inherent *sortedness* in already sorted or near-sorted data to reduce the ingestion cost, rather, ends up doing *extra* work in establishing order in data that already had some degree of inherent sortedness. Thus, regardless of the data sortedness, PostgreSQL ends up spending $\sim 20\times$ ($108\,\mu s$) more time during data ingestion through individual insertions compared to the bulk loading time.

**Column-Store Systems Require a Fundamental Redesign to Support Data Sortedness.** Most column-store systems primarily optimize for the read performance of analytical queries through vertical partitioning, vectorization, compression, tight for-loops, and cache efficiency and do not rely on secondary indexes [1]. Further, when loading data, one cannot enforce the system to maintain the data fully sorted (similar to what a secondary B-tree index would do in a row-store), hence, column-store systems would require fundamental design changes to try and accommodate a variable degree of data sortedness. For example, MonetDB supports two types of indexes, *imprints* [17] and *ordered indexes* (essentially a sorted version of the desired columns), which are both invalidated after any insert, update, or delete on the corresponding tables [15]. We run workloads A and B on MonetDB using the ordered index with auto-commit off. As we vary the underlying sortedness for each workload, we observe that the runtime does not change since we only pay the cost of vertically partitioning the incom-

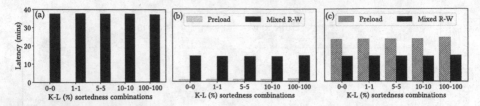

**Fig. 7.** Performance of PostgreSQL with mixed workloads: (a) Mixed workload with no pre-loading (b) Mixed workload using bulk loading for preloading (c) Mixed workload using individual inserts for preloading.

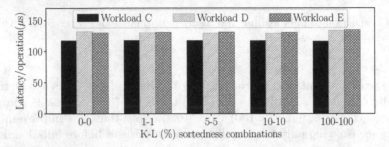

**Fig. 8.** Comparison of latency per operation among the mixed workloads C, D and E.

ing data and populating the table's columns. Note that the index is invalidated after the first update and is not maintained thereafter.

We now briefly discuss two commercial column-store systems, Vertica and Actian Vector. Vertica supports *projections*, which are similar to ordered indexes and do not support live updates [13]. Hence, we expect to have similar behavior to MonetDB. Actian Vector supports live updates in a sorted column through an approach called Positional Delta Tree (PDT) [11]. PDT is essentially a variation of an in-memory B-tree with positional information. Hence, based on our experimentation with an in-memory B-tree [16], we do not expect significant performance differences when varying sortedness. However, more experimentation is needed to fully assess Vertica's and Actian Vector's capability to exploit sortedness, which we leave as future work.

## 5.2   Mixed Workload Performance

In this set of experiments, we compare the performance of PostgreSQL under the three mixed workload settings supported by our benchmark: (i) mixed with no preloading (workload C); (ii) mixed after bulk load (workload D); and (iii) mixed after individual insertions (workload E). For workload C, we perform 16M insertions interleaved uniformly with 3.2M point queries, while for the workloads D and E we first preload the system with 12.8M data rows and then perform 3.2M inserts interleaved uniformly with 3.2M point queries. Again, the *preloading phase* is written to an intermediary file `preload.sql` that is either empty (for

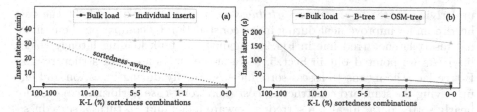

**Fig. 9.** (a) A sortedness-aware system should adapt to data characteristics. (b) OSM-tree index is an example of an index that adapts to data sortedness to offer favorable ingestion.

workload C) or contains a `COPY` command (for workload D) or 12.8M `INSERT` statements (for workload E); while in the *operations phase* the `operations.sql` file contains the interleaved `INSERT` and `SELECT` statements. We then execute both files on PostgreSQL and measure the workload execution latency. Figure 7 shows the comparison of phase-wise execution time for all three workloads.

**PostgreSQL Cannot Harness Sortedness as a Resource.** When ingesting a mixed workload with uniformly interleaved reads and writes, even for a completely sorted data collection ($K = L = 0$) the performance of PostgreSQL mimics the performance of ingesting unsorted data ($K = L = 100$), as seen from Fig. 7(a). When performing individual insertions, the underlying B-tree index is unable to identify if the ingested data is completely sorted. This is because state-of-the-art index structures lack a mechanism to assess data sortedness of ingested entries on the fly. In fact, this trend can also be observed in the operational latency for workload D, as well as both phase-wise latencies in workload E.

Figure 8 shows the average latency-per-operation for mixed workloads C, D, and E as we vary the data sortedness. While the average operational latency remains largely unaffected by data sortedness, we observe that workload C shows ~15-16% lower latency as compared to mixed workloads D and E. Workload C contains no preloading phase, and hence, initial operations are performed on a smaller database (and subsequently, a smaller index) by size. On the other hand, workloads D and E do contain a preloading phase where the database and index are warmed-up with 3.2 GB data (80% of 4 GB), and thus, every insert or query needs to traverse the index which exacerbates the operational cost. Note that workload C represents the initialization-state of the index/database, while workloads D and E represent the steady-state.

## 6 Toward Sortedness Awareness

From our experiments with PostgreSQL, we have observed that the system is *unsurprisingly* not sortedness-aware. Figure 9a summarizes the results from Sect. 5, where we maintain a B-tree index during data ingestion with increasing sortedness. PostgreSQL is agnostic to sortedness due to the inability of the underlying B-tree to *use data sortedness as a resource*. We highlight the vast headroom for improvement during index construction by comparing the individual insert latency (red line in Fig. 9a) against the bulk loading latency (black line). As we pointed out in Sect. 5, state-of-the-art index data structures like B-tree lack the means to assess sortedness on the fly during ingestion and end up paying the standard construction cost (i.e., worst-case performance) even for nearly sorted data. Ideally, a sortedness-aware index and, in turn, a sortedness-aware system should *lower the index construction cost* when ingesting data with increasing sortedness and, thus, follow a trend similar to the dotted blue line in Fig. 9a.

Existing literature on indexes does not explore sortedness when optimizing index construction. Providing classical indexes with the means to capture data sortedness during ingestion (most notably, buffering) would incur a read overhead. Hence, we expect a tradeoff between optimizing index construction by harnessing data sortedness and read performance. However, an ideal sortedness-aware index should be able to navigate this performance tradeoff. It should offer near-optimal ingestion (bulk loading) in the presence of high data sortedness, while falling back to the current baseline otherwise. Further, it should amortize any read overheads incurred to offer better overall performance. A first design that uses sortedness as a resource is the OSM-tree [16] which uses a buffer to capture data sortedness in memory and to maximize bulk loading. Figure 9b shows that the OSM-tree acts like a B-tree when ingesting unsorted data (left-end of the x-axis), and mimics bulk loading when ingesting fully sorted data (right-end of the x-axis), while bridging the gap for data sortedness between the two extremes. Similarly to the experiments with PostgreSQL, we ingest 16M keys and allocate a buffer pool of 25% of the total data size to both OSM-tree and B-tree. We use workload A for the bulk loading line, and workload B for the individual inserts to the B-tree and the OSM-tree, to which we allocate an in-memory buffer of 1% of the total data size. This small in-memory buffer investment, along with the other design elements of OSM-tree (e.g., partial opportunistic bulk loading), leads to ~9× faster ingestion for fully sorted data, making individual inserts almost as efficient as bulk loading. Even for lower data sortedness ($K = L = 10\%$), OSM-tree offers a ~5× improvement over B-tree, while mimicking the baseline for unsorted data. Overall, having a sortedness-aware design will allow data systems to build their indexes faster, e.g., via batching inserts that can be opportunistically bulk loaded. Such a sortedness-aware system may offer orders of magnitude better ingestion performance in the presence of data sortedness, which will be beneficial even for mixed read/write workloads.

# 7   Conclusion

The Benchmark on Data Sortedness lays the groundwork to test systems and index data structures that will be designed to harness data sortedness. We expect the trend shown in Fig. 9 to match the observed performance for sortedness-aware indexing data structures and systems, with variations that will correspond to the degree each approach is optimized for interleaving reads and writes, accurately capturing sortedness, and memory availability. Overall, we expect that new sortedness-aware data structure designs and data systems will emerge and will employ BoDS to show how they cope with variable data sortedness.

**Acknowledgements.** This work is funded by NSF Grants IIS-2144547 and IIS-1850202, a Facebook Faculty Research Award, and a Meta gift.

# References

1. Abadi, D.J., Boncz, P.A., Harizopoulos, S.: Column-oriented database systems. Proc. VLDB Endowment **2**(2), 1664–1665 (2009). https://doi.org/10.14778/1687553.1687625
2. Achakeev, D., Seeger, B.: Efficient bulk updates on Multiversion B-trees. Proc. VLDB Endowment **6**(14), 1834–1845 (2013). https://doi.org/10.14778/2556549.2556566
3. Athanassoulis, M., Ailamaki, A.: BF-Tree: approximate tree indexing. Proc. VLDB Endowment **7**(14), 1881–1892 (2014). http://www.vldb.org/pvldb/vol7/p1881-athanassoulis.pdf
4. Athanassoulis, M., Yan, Z., Idreos, S.: UpBit: scalable In-memory updatable bitmap indexing. In: Proceedings of the ACM SIGMOD International Conference on Management of Data (2016). https://dl.acm.org/citation.cfm?id=2915964
5. Ben-Moshe, S., Kanza, Y., Fischer, E., Matsliah, A., Fischer, M., Staelin, C.: Detecting and exploiting near-sortedness for efficient relational query evaluation. In: Proceedings of the International Conference on Database Theory (ICDT), pp. 256–267 (2011). https://doi.org/10.1145/1938551.1938584
6. Bender, M.A., et al.: An introduction to Bε-trees and write-optimization. White Paper (2015). http://supertech.csail.mit.edu/papers/BenderFaJa15.pdf
7. den Bercken, J.V., Seeger, B.: An evaluation of generic bulk loading techniques. In: Proceedings of the International Conference on Very Large Data Bases (VLDB), pp. 461–470 (2001). http://www.vldb.org/conf/2001/P461.pdf
8. Carlsson, S., Chen, J.: On partitions and presortedness of sequences. Acta Informatica **29**, 267–280 (1992). https://doi.org/10.1007/BF01185681
9. Graefe, G.: B-tree indexes, interpolation search, and skew. In: Proceedings of the International Workshop on Data Management on New Hardware (DAMON) (2006). http://dl.acm.org/citation.cfm?id=1140402.1140409
10. Graefe, G.: Modern B-tree techniques. Found. Trends Databases **3**(4), 203–402 (2011). https://doi.org/10.1561/1900000028
11. Héman, S., Zukowski, M., Nes, N.J.: Positional Update Handling in Column Stores. In: Proceedings of the ACM SIGMOD International Conference on Management of Data, pp. 543–554 (2010), http://dl.acm.org/citation.cfm?id=1807167.1807227
12. Knuth, D.E.: The art of computer programming, Volume I: Fundamental Algorithms (3rd Edition). Addison-Wesley (1997). http://www.worldcat.org/oclc/312910844
13. Lamb, A., Fuller, M., Varadarajan, R.: The vertica analytic database: C-Store 7 years later. Proc. VLDB Endowment **5**(12), 1790–1801 (2012). http://dl.acm.org/citation.cfm?id=2367518
14. Mannila, H.: Measures of Presortedness and optimal sorting algorithms. IEEE Trans. Comput. (TC) **34**(4), 318–325 (1985). https://doi.org/10.1109/TC.1985.5009382

15. MonetDB: Index Definitions (2022). https://www.monetdb.org/documentation-Jan2022/user-guide/sql-manual/data-definition/index-definitions/
16. Raman, A., Sarkar, S., Olma, M., Athanassoulis, M.: OSM-tree: a sortedness-aware index. CoRR abs/2202.0 (2022). https://doi.org/10.48550/arXiv.2202.04185, https://arxiv.org/abs/2202.04185
17. Sidirourgos, L., Kersten, M.L.: Column imprints: a secondary index structure. In: Proceedings of the ACM SIGMOD International Conference on Management of Data, pp. 893–904 (2013). http://dl.acm.org/citation.cfm?id=2463676.2465306
18. Stonebraker, M.: The case for partial indexes. ACM SIGMOD Rec. **18**(4), 4–11 (1989). https://doi.org/10.1145/74120.74121
19. TPC: TPC-H benchmark (2021). http://www.tpc.org/tpch/

# Disaggregated Database Management Systems

Shahram Ghandeharizadeh[1]([✉]), Philip A. Bernstein[2], Dhruba Borthakur[3],
Haoyu Huang[4], Jai Menon[5], and Sumit Puri[6]

[1] USC, Los Angeles, CA, USA
shahram@usc.edu
[2] Microsoft Research, Redmond, WA, USA
phil.bernstein@microsoft.com
[3] Rockset, San Mateo, CA, USA
dhruba@rockset.com
[4] Google, Mountain View, CA, USA
haoyuhuang@google.com
[5] Fungible, Santa Clara, CA, USA
jai.menon@fungible.com
[6] Liqid, Broomfield, CO, USA
sumit@liqid.com

**Abstract.** Modern applications demand high performance and cost efficient database management systems (DBMSs). Their workloads may
be diverse, ranging from online transaction processing to analytics and
decision support. The cloud infrastructure enables disaggregation of
monolithic DBMSs into components that facilitate software-hardware co-
design. This is realized using pools of hardware resources, i.e., CPUs,
GPUs, memory, FPGA, NVM, etc., connected using high-speed networks.
This disaggregation trend is being adopted by cloud DBMSs because hardware re-provisioning can be achieved by simply invoking software APIs.
Disaggregated DBMSs separate processing from storage, enabling each
to scale elastically and independently. They may disaggregate compute
usage based on functionality, e.g., compute needed for writes from compute needed for queries and compute needed for compaction. They may
also use disaggregated memory, e.g., for intermediate results in a shuffle or
for remote caching. The DBMS monitors the characteristics of a workload
and dynamically assembles its components that are most efficient and cost
effective for the workload. This paper is a summary of a panel session that
discussed the capability, challenges, and opportunities of these emerging
DBMSs and disaggregated hardware systems.

## 1 Introduction

Emerging data centers disaggregate hardware into pools of resources and connect them using fast networks such as high-speed Ethernet or Remote Direct
Memory Access, RDMA [10]. The pool of resources may include CPUs, GPUs,
memory, NVMe, disks, SSDs, FPGAs, and specialized hardware such as Amazon Trainium and Google TPU for machine learning among others. The software

R. Nambiar and M. Poess (Eds.): TPCTC 2022, LNCS 13860, pp. 33–48, 2023.
https://doi.org/10.1007/978-3-031-29576-8_3

that implements a database management system may also be disaggregated into micro-services. Both trends facilitate a software-hardware co-design. Moreover, they enable composition of micro-services into new services. For example, an in-memory key-value store may be realized using a subset of micro-services that implement a relational database management system (DBMS) [6]. Assembly of the components must consider the communication latency and employ caches to prevent this latency from dominating performance.

Disaggregated DBMSs hold the potential to transform today's obsolete practices to enhance efficiency by providing sustainable solutions. Instead of asking a user to size a server, they may ask a user for their daily budget and desired performance objective. Now, it is the responsibility of an intelligent agent to assemble the hardware and software to meet the price and performance requirements. With a high (low) system load, the assembled system may scale-up (down). The system may use alternative forms of storage that provide different price/performance characteristics [7].

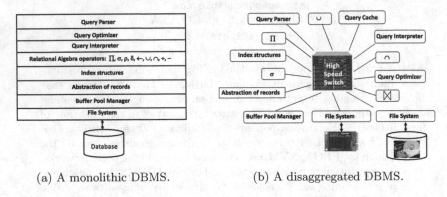

(a) A monolithic DBMS.                    (b) A disaggregated DBMS.

**Fig. 1.** Today's monolithic DBMS and the envisioned disaggregated DBMS.

Physical data design is a task performed by data administrators to enhance efficiency and meet the performance requirements of an application. They make decisions such as whether the data is stored in a column format or a row format. However, many startups do not have a budget to pay these experts, resulting in inefficiencies. A disaggregated DBMS will address this by monitoring the system workload and fine-tuning the physical design of the database, choice of hardware including a storage hierarchy, and microservices assembled to realize the most cost effective deployment.

Today's use of data centers by scientists, including those in the area of machine learning and AI, requires them to upload their data to a data center and run their computation in the cloud. A key question is what data to copy to the cloud? As an example, NIH's-National Library of Medicine has 36.4 Petabytes of Genomic sequencing data on two commercial cloud platforms [15]. How are scientists to discover and use this data? Scientists want to know what is the minimum cost configuration for an experiment. They may have a fixed budget for running an experiment. Once the budget is exhausted, they may want to save their result files and have the service shut-down so there are no additional charges [15]. They may also want to take a snapshot of their mid-flight experiment that enables them to continue where it was stopped.

A vision for a future system is one that reduces data movement and replication [15]. One way to realize this is to extend the disaggregation beyond a data center to include a scientist's desktop. It provides for physical data independence, a concept pioneered by the database community, where the scientist is no longer burdened with the placement of data. It is the responsibility of the infrastructure to manage placement of data and computation seamlessly.

The rest of this paper is organized as follows. Sections 2, 3 and 4 describe hardware, memory, and DBMS disaggregation in turn. Brief future research directions are presented in Sect. 5.

## 2    Hardware Disaggregation

Storage, GPUs, memory, and other hardware resources are traditionally included as part of a traditional server. A limitation of this organization is the box that contains these resources. Success is effectively limited to what can fit in a box. To obtain enough of a critical resource, customers are forced to purchase larger, more expensive servers than required for new deployments or remove and replace a server when that critical resource is maxed-out.

Disaggregating the hardware resources from the servers allows for much better utilization of these resources. There are three questions to answer when disaggregating resources: Which hardware resources are being disaggregated? What bus, fabric, or network to use to connect the disaggregated resources? And, what is the performance impact of disaggregation? Consider each question in turn.

**What Hardware Resources are Being Disaggregated?** Storage has been disaggregated for many years. Storage products that disaggregate at the file level (NAS) and at the block level (SAN) have been available for several decades.

GPUs and memory have not been disaggregated until very recently. Products that disaggregate GPUs have become available in the last year. Memory disaggregation is emerging.

**What Fabric is Used for Disaggregation?** Storage disaggregation has been accomplished using Fiber Channel (FC), Ethernet, and InfiniBand (IB). Protocols such as SCSI over FC, NFS over Ethernet and SCSI over Ethernet (iSCSI) have been employed for this purpose. An emerging approach is NVMeoF for block level disaggregation. See https://nvmexpress.org/wp-content/uploads/ NVMe_Over_Fabrics.pdf for details. GPU disaggregation has been realized using PCIe Fabrics and over Ethernet. Memory disaggregation is being attempted over emerging buses such as CXL (https://www.computeexpresslink.org/). It is also possible over Ethernet.

**What is the Performance Impact of Disaggregation?** Disaggregation improves resource utilization, but it may result in some performance loss. The closer the performance of the disaggregated resource is to its performance when locally attached to the server, the more likely it is that disaggregation is employed.

There is a tradeoff between using fabrics that allow data center wide disaggregation (such as Ethernet) and those that support disaggregation over shorter distances. It is harder to achieve good performance over data center wide distances. However, customers like the flexibility offered by disaggregation at scale.

With new protocols such as NVMeoF, disaggregated storage performance close to that of server attached storage has been demonstrated, even at data center scale. Similarly, new approaches have also shown that disaggregated GPU performance can be anywhere from 80% to 99% of local GPU performance at data center scale over Ethernet.

The next two sections present two approaches to hardware disaggregation.

## 2.1 Fungible's DPU-Based Disaggregation

A DPU (data processing unit) is a specialized programmable processor tailored to efficiently execute data-centric tasks. These are tasks that require stateful processing simultaneously on multiple high bandwidth streams of data. An increasing fraction of work done in modern data centers is data centric in nature, and CPUs and GPUs are inefficient at such tasks. Disaggregation is essentially a data centric task and DPUs have proven to be very efficient at disaggregation. As a result, an emerging trend is the use of DPUs for hardware disaggregation.

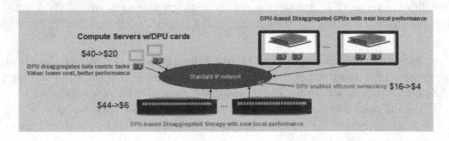

**Fig. 2.** DPU-based disaggregated data center using standard IP networks.

Fungible has built 2 DPUs [14], one small enough to fit on a PCIe card inside a server, a second one powerful enough to build a disaggregated storage system.

Using the DPU, Fungible has built a disaggregated storage system with performance indistinguishable from that of server attached storage. This system is called the Fungible Storage Cluster (FSC).

It has also built a DPU-based PCIe card that plugs into the PCIe slot of a standard server and disaggregates networking, security and storage functions transparently from the server. This allows server cores to be dedicated to running applications instead of being used inefficiently to run infrastructure tasks.

Finally, it has developed a DPU-based disaggregated GPU appliance with performance between 80–99% of server attached GPUs. Customers can now run AI/ML on servers without any GPUs, and they have the flexibility to change the mix of CPU cores and GPU cores applied to a given problem.

Fungible's vision of the next-generation data center is shown in Fig. 2. All servers have DPU based cards. Storage and GPUs are disaggregated and are built with DPUs. The result is a data center that costs about 30% of one without DPU-based disaggregation. It allows the disaggregated components to be dynamically composed on the fly to meet workload needs for great agility.

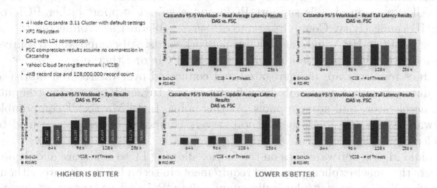

**Fig. 3.** Cassandra DBMS: Fungible FSC vs. DAS.

Figure 3 shows the performance of Fungible's disaggregated storage system versus server attached storage, also known as Direct Attached Storage (DAS), for a database workload and shows that performance is indistinguishable.

Additional details on Fungible's storage offering using DPUs can be found in [12,13].

## 2.2 Liqid's Composable Disaggregated Infrastructure (CDI)

Composable Disaggregated Infrastructure (CDI) solutions add a software component to hardware disaggregation. CDI solutions consist of three parts: the disaggregated hardware components, a fabric that connects the disaggregated hardware components, and software (sometimes referred to as a composer) that allows for dynamically configuring the hardware components to create hardware infrastructure that precisely matches workload needs.

Instead of physically ordering hardware infrastructure with the required cores, memory, GPUs and Storage, CDI can dynamically compose and deploy such infrastructure in minutes.

Liqid CDI disaggregates a datacenter's infrastructure using PCIe-deployed devices. This includes GPU's, FPGA's, SSD's, and Storage Class Memory. NIC's are not installed in the server chassis. Instead, they are disaggregated, and placed into external PCIe enclosures, called expansion chassis.

An organization can have as many expansion chassis as are required to hold their storage, accelerators, and/or networking resources. Liqid is vendor agnostic enabling customers to choose what resources they compose. Visit https://www.liqid.com/resources/all for details.

Liqid's composable fabric switch then interconnects all the resources to be composed, providing every composable resource direct access to each other. For connections between chassis and racks to be transparent to workloads, Liqid leverages high bandwidth technology, including PCIe (Gen 4 and Gen 3). While Liqid also supports Ethernet and InfiniBand (Eth/IB) fabrics, they are not covered in the scope of this document.

Organizations choose the fabric type that best meets their composability requirements and can even create multi-fabric environments that support them all. All expansion chassis support PCIe and a subset support either PCIe or Eth/IB connectivity. Compute resources (servers/blades) are connected to the fabric via PCIe HBA and/ or 100GbE network cards. All composable resources connected to high-speed fabric switches, either PCIe or Ethernet.

Once resources are disaggregated and connected over distributed fabric(s), the data center has essentially been flattened and turned into massive computing, accelerator, and storage pools. At this point, Liqid Matrix$^{TM}$ composable software is used to create bare metal servers composed of resources tuned to meet any workload need, in seconds.

Liqid Matrix software lives on the fabric, allowing IT to configure and deploy servers that meet explicit workload requirements in seconds via software without worrying if a server can physically support its GPU and or storage resources. If demand increases, add more resources on-demand. As compute needs evolve, unused resources can be reclaimed for use by other applications. Liqid Matrix CDI software enables organizations to:

- Accelerate time-to-results with right-sized systems, deployed real-time via software;
- Adapt in real-time to evolving business needs with a zerotouch, change-ready agility;
- Drive new levels of efficiency with superior resource utilization and an as-a-service approach to infrastructure;
- Save on capital and operational expenses while providing a dynamic, disaggregated infrastructure that is part of a more sustainable, software-defined data center ecosystem.

Liqid has seen adoption for the following use cases:

- AI+ML & data science: Accelerate time-to-research for scientists by enabling them to tailor systems that meet challenging workload needs in seconds, rather than forcing them to manually configure servers and accelerators.
- HPC: Get answers to today's most urgent questions faster by composing previously impossible server configurations for HPC. Quickly deploy systems with precise amounts of GPU, accelerator, storage, and networking, eliminating the need to manually install or remove components from the server chassis.

- End user computing: Meet the most demanding virtual desktop infrastructure (VDI) requirements with Liqid CDI. Compose only what's needed to meet today's desktop requirements and then scale GPU resources up or down via software as workload demands dictate.
- Server virtualization: Extend the flexibility of virtualization to VMware ESX host servers with Liqid CDI. Quickly compose bare-metal host servers that meet precise workload requirements all via the Liqid vCenter Plug-in. No longer is GPU performance capacity limited by what can fit in a server. Increase VM and workload density with Liqid.
- Edge computing: Cameras, sensors, and cell phones will continue to create vast amounts of data; edge compute is increasingly needed to process that data quickly. Liqid composability creates flexible configurations that make edge deployments a reality. Liqid is uniquely suited to address common edge challenges including limited power, floor space, cooling and human access.

Software-defined CDI enables IT organizations to reap cloud-like speed and flexibility in their own core and edge infrastructure.

## 3   Memory Disaggregation

Stateful on-line applications maintain a large amount of data and require fast processing times. Examples include interactive games, fraud detection, and social networking, among others. These applications cache their data in memory to provide fast response time. If main memory were free, these applications would cache all their data in memory. However, memory is not free. Moreover, each server in the cloud has a limited amount of memory to offer an application. This limitation is exacerbated during peak system load of a stateful service when it requires additional memory to meet its Service Level Objective (SLO).

Today's data centers are awash in unused main memory [19,20]. By some estimates, more than 50% of data center memory is either un-allocated or unused at any given time [4,17]. One reason for this is the over-provisioning a virtual machine (VM) to handle the occasional VM resize operation without requiring a VM migration. Another is external fragmentation when VMs allocated on a host machine leave insufficient resources to allocate another VM of a useful size.

A disaggregated hardware platform provides fast networking to enable data management systems, DMSs[1], to access remote memory with acceptable latency, enhancing overall memory utilization. In [19], we present an elastic memory management system named Redy. Redy tunes RDMA in a particular deployment to satisfy a user-provided SLO and minimize resource cost.

A future research direction is how to size the server-local memory cache to satisfy the required latency and throughput of a workload. This depends on the cache miss rate as a function of cache size and the latency of servicing a cache miss. The former depends on the degree of skew of references to data which in

---

[1] A DMS includes traditional relational database management systems, key-value stores, document stores, etc.

turn dictates the placement of data. The latter depends on the type of storage that services the miss. Example storage include remote memory, server-local disk, or cloud storage. This research direction may benefit from open industry standards such as Compute Express Link (CXL) for CPU-to-memory connections. CXL is designed for high performance data center computers and provides cache-coherent protocols for accessing system memory (CXL.cache) and device memory (CXL.mem), and block input/output protocol (CXL.io).

# 4   Disaggregated Database Management Systems

## 4.1   AlloyDB

Today's applications have high demand on database performance and stringent service level agreement (SLA) requirements. An SLA may require a database to provide high throughput with a $90^{th}$ percentile response time less than a given threshold, e.g., 100 milliseconds. Applications also have a high velocity. They want to perform complex analytics on fresh data to provide the latest business insights.

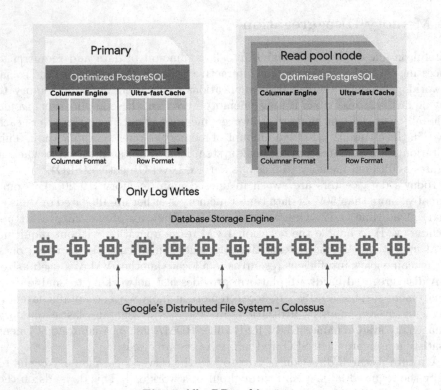

**Fig. 4.** AlloyDB architecture.

AlloyDB is a new enterprise grade SQL database product that aims at meeting those application demands. It combines PostgreSQL with compute-storage disaggregation, read pools for horizontal scalability, and HTAP support. Figure 4 shows the architecture of AlloyDB, with the primary database instance, a set of read pools, and an intelligent, distributed storage engine as the key building blocks. AlloyDB disaggregates the primary and read pools from the database storage engine and enables each layer to scale independently of the others. An AlloyDB cluster consists of one primary and multiple read pools. A read pool consists of multiple read replicas. The storage engine persists data in the distributed file system, Colossus.

Read pools isolate performance for different workloads of an application. An application may categorize its workloads and issue queries from the same category to the same read pool. For example, a wholesale retailer may create three read pools for its web sales, store sales, and catalog sales. This ensures that read queries for web sales are isolated from the queries for store sales.

Read pools also provide horizontal scalability. A read pool balances the load across its replicas. An application may scale the number of replicas in a read pool dynamically based on the system load. The scaling is elastic and does not require moving data in the storage engine. When the system load becomes high, an application may create additional replicas to shed load. It may reduce the number of replicas in a pool when the load dials down.

To provide fast query response time for both transactional and analytical queries, the primary and replicas employ an ultra-fast row cache and a pluggable columnar engine. The row cache caches the working set in row-oriented format while the columnar engine caches them in column-oriented format. Columnar engine uses single instruction, multiple data (SIMD) vectorization to facilitate query processing. It also monitors the workload and automatically columnarizes data to maximize performance. The primary and replicas process a query using the columnar engine, the cached data in row format, or a hybrid of two.

AlloyDB's storage engine is further disaggregated into several components to provide high performance. It also decouples durability from availability, see Fig. 5. AlloyDB stores log records durably in the regional log storage and the database in the regional block storage, Colossus. The log storage optimizes for append-only log operations to reduce the transaction commit latency. To ensure all blocks are readily available for primary and replicas, the storage engine uses multiple log processing servers (LPS) that ingest log records and materialize blocks from log records continuously. LPS materializes the blocks in the same zones as the primary and replicas. They are purely compute-attached to a shared regional storage and can flexibly scale without needing to copy any data. Internally, AlloyDB scales up the number of LPSs when the system load is high to provide consistent performance. It scales down during low system load to reduce cost. The storage engine also handles the backup operations completely and does not impact the performance and resources of the compute layer.

AlloyDB also adopts a component-based architecture. It offers rich functionalities through multiple extensions to PostgreSQL. For example, the columnar engine extension plugs into the query optimizer and query execution to facilitate query processing. The database advisor extension provides physical database

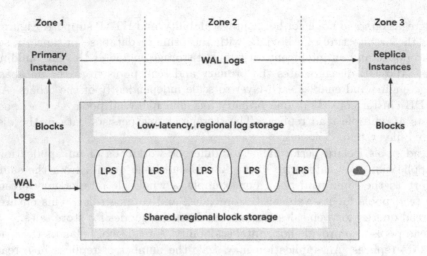

**Fig. 5.** AlloyDB storage engine.

design recommendations based on the workload, e.g., indexes, and the query insights extension offers observability into the query performance. AlloyDB also supports widely used PostgreSQL extensions from the open-source community.

### 4.2  Rockset

**Real-Time Databases Demand Disaggregation:** This section describes a disaggregated architecture for realtime databases. We examine, in detail, Rockset, which is a real-time analytics database service for processing low latency, highly concurrent analytical queries at scale. Rockset builds a Converged Index$^{TM}$ on structured and semi-structured data from OLTP databases, streams and lakes in real-time and exposes a RESTful SQL interface. We first discuss the requirements of a disaggregated architecture for powering realtime data applications. We then explain why the Aggregator Leaf Architecture (ALT) is able to power realtime data applications. Finally, we present how Rockset disaggregates the RocksDB architecture to separate compute from storage.

Many applications are powered by realtime databases. Examples include food ordered and tracked online, Facebook or LinkedIn's newsfeed, and others. These applications require real-time analytics to provide interactive user requests with fresh data. This means fast queries with sub-second response times. New events are streamed into the database at hundreds of megabytes a second. Fresh data means new data becomes visible to queries within a few seconds of it being updated. The update rate to the database is inherently bursty in nature and, at the same time, these realtime data applications demand that queries are not impacted by bursty writes. This motivates processing of the writes to be sepa-

rated from the processing of reads. This is the primary reason why disaggregation is key to powering realtime databases. Aggregator Leaf Tailer (ALT) is the
disaggregated data architecture favored by web-scale companies, like Facebook,
LinkedIn, and Google, for its efficiency and scalability for powering realtime
applications.

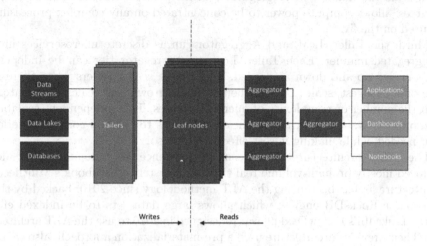

**Fig. 6.** Aggregator Leaf Tailer Architecture (ALT)

**The Aggregator Leaf Tailer Disaggregated Architecture (ALT):** The
ALT architecture [1] is a design pattern for realtime databases, see Fig. 6. This
architecture facilitates a three way disaggregation among the compute required
for writes, the compute required for reads, and the storage required to store
and retrieve the data. The salient features of the ALT architecture include the
following. First, the Tailer pulls new incoming data from a static or streaming
source into an indexing engine. Its job is to fetch from all data sources, be it a
data lake, like S3, or a dynamic source, like Kafka or Kinesis. Second, the Leaf
is a powerful indexing engine. It indexes all data as it arrives via the Tailer. The
indexing component builds multiple types of indexes—inverted, columnar, document, geo, and many others—on the fields of a data set. Its indexes expedite
processing of queries that reference a data field. Third, the scalable Aggregator
tier is designed to deliver low-latency aggregations, be it columnar aggregations,
joins, relevance sorting, or grouping. The Aggregators leverage indexing so efficiently that complex logic typically executed by data-pipeline software in other
architectures can be executed on the fly as a part of the query.

The ALT architecture enables the application developer to run low-latency
queries on raw data sets with minor prior transformation. A large portion of the
data transformation process occurs as a part of the query itself. There are three
reasons why this is possible. First, indexing is critical to making queries fast. The
Leaves, see Fig. 6, maintain a variety of indexes concurrently, so that relevant

data can be accessed quickly regardless of the type of query—aggregation, key-value, time series, or search. Every document and field is indexed, including both value and type of each field, resulting in fast query performance that allows significantly more complex data processing to be inserted into queries.

Second, Queries are distributed across a scalable Aggregator tier. The ability to scale the number of Aggregators, which provide compute and memory resources, allows compute power to be concentrated on any complex processing executed on the fly.

Third, the Tailer, Leaf, and Aggregator run as discrete microservices in a disaggregated manner. Each Tailer, Leaf, or Aggregator tier can be independently scaled up and down as needed. The system scales Tailers when there is more data to ingest, scales Leaves when data size grows, and scales Aggregators when the number or complexity of queries increases. This independent scalability allows the system to bring significant resources to bear on complex queries when needed, while making it cost-effective to do so.

The ALT architecture has been in existence for almost a decade, employed mostly on high-volume real-time data systems. Facebook's Multifeed Architecture [5] has been using the ALT methodology since 2010, backed by the open-source RocksDB engine, which allows large data sets to be indexed efficiently. LinkedIn's FollowFeed [9] was redesigned in 2016 to use the ALT architecture. Their previous architecture used a pre-materialization approach, also called fan-out-on-write, where results were precomputed and made available for simple lookup queries. LinkedIn's new ALT architecture uses a query on demand or fan-out-on-read model using RocksDB indexing instead of Lucene indexing. Much of the computation is done on the fly, allowing greater speed and flexibility for developers in this approach. Rockset uses RocksDB as a foundational data store and implements the ALT architecture [16] in a cloud service.

**Disaggregation of Compaction CPU in RocksDB in the Cloud:** Rockset uses RocksDB-Cloud as one of the building blocks of its distributed Converged Index. Rockset is designed with cloud-native principles, and one of the primary design principles of a cloud-native database is to separate compute from storage. Below, we describe how Rockset extends RocksDB-Cloud to realize this separation. This is open source software and may be adopted by other realtime databases.

RocksDB-Cloud stores data in locally attached SSD or spinning disks. New writes to RocksDB-Cloud are written to an in-memory memtable. Once the memtable is full, it is flushed to a new SST file in the storage. Being an LSM storage engine, a set of background threads are used for compaction. Compaction is a process of combining a set of SST files and generating new SST files with overwritten keys and deleted keys purged from the new files. Compaction is a compute intensive task. It requires more resources with a higher rate of writes to the database, enabling the system to keep up with the new writes. See Fig. 7.

In a typical RocksDB-based system using a shared-nothing architecture [2, 18], compaction occurs on CPUs that are local on the server that also hosts

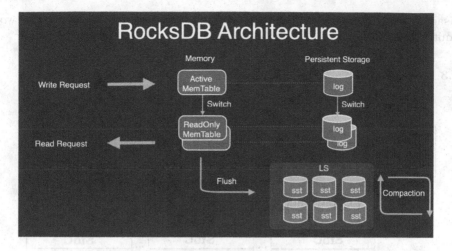

**Fig. 7.** RocksDB

the storage. In this case, compute and storage are not disaggregated. Hence, if the write rate increases while the total size of the database remains unchanged, the system provisions more servers to process writes. It spreads the data across these additional servers and uses their compute resources to keep up with the compaction load. This shared-nothing approach suffers from the following two limitations: First, Re-organizing data across additional servers is not instantaneous. If the workload changes during the re-organization process then the system may not benefit from the additional servers. Second, The utilization of storage capacity is lowered because the database size did not change. However, it is spread across additional servers with more storage. This lowers price-to-performance ratio due to unused storage on the servers.

Next, we describe how Rockset addresses these two limitations by separating compute from storage using disaggregated RocksDB-Cloud. The primary reason why RocksDB-Cloud is suitable for separating out compaction compute and storage is because it is an LSM storage engine. Unlike a B-Tree database, RocksDB-Cloud never updates an SST file once it is created. This means that all the SST files in the entire system are read-only except the miniscule portion of data in the active memtable. RocksDB-Cloud persists all SST files in a cloud storage object store such as Amazon S3. These cloud objects are safely accessible from all the servers because they are read-only. Thus, a RocksDB-Cloud server A may encapsulate a compaction job with its set of cloud objects and send the request to a remote stateless server B. Server B fetches the relevant objects from the cloud store, compacts them, writes a set of output SST files back to the cloud object store, and notifies server A that the compaction job is complete. In essence, the storage (which resides in server A) is separated from the compaction compute (which resides in server B). Server A has the storage and while server B has no permanent storage but only the compute needed for compaction. This disaggregation is superior to the shared-nothing approach by eliminating its two limitations.

### 4.3  Nova-LSM

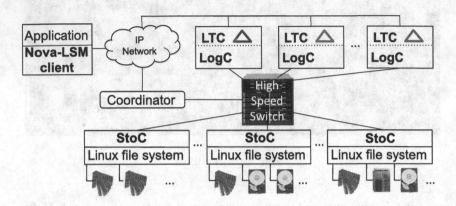

**Fig. 8.** Architecture.

Nova-LSM is a distributed LSM-tree key-value store that disaggregates storage from processing [11]. Figure 8 shows its architecture, consisting of LSM-tree components (LTC), logging components (LogC), and storage components (StoC). These components are connected using a high speed RDMA network. Application data is range partitioned across LTCs and each LTC is assigned several ranges. An LTC maintains one LSM-tree for each of its assigned ranges and processes application requests using these trees. LogC maintains log records of a LSM-tree and is integrated into LTC. It generates log records when processing writes. It also fetches log records to recover a LSM-tree. StoC stores, retrieves, and manages blocks. A StoC may consist of main memory (DRAM), non-volatile memory, disk, or a hierarchy of these storage devices. It leverages one-sided RDMA read/write primitives to provide high performance.

A StoC may implement compaction as data is shared across all StoCs. An LTC may write data to any StoC. Each write request uses power-of-d to dynamically selects the fastest StoC. The coordinator maintains the assignment of ranges to LTCs to balance load. In [11], we present experimental results showing Nova-LSM provides 10x higher throughput than RocksDB [3] and LevelDB [8].

Nova-LSM is elastic. It may scale its number of StoCs and LTCs dynamically based on system load. When LTCs are fully utilizes, Nova-LSM may construct additional LTCs to shed load without the need to move data across StoCs. A new LTC is assigned one or more ranges and constructs its LSM-tree metadata to process client requests referencing its ranges. The LSM-tree reads data stored in a StoC. Figure 9 shows the throughput of a system as we increase and decrease the number of LTCs. The starting configuration consists of 1 LTC and 13 StoCs.

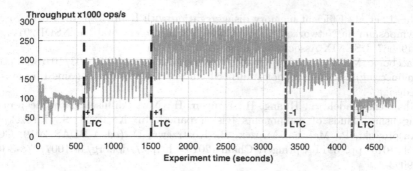

**Fig. 9.** Nova-LSM is elastic. LTCs and StoCs may scale independently.

Its peak throughput is 100,000 operations per second with the CPU cores of 1 LTC fully utilized. An increase in the system load motivates an increase in the number of LTCs, causing the peak throughput to increase linearly as the new LTCs process requests and reduce the load on the bottleneck LTC. As the system load decreases, the number of LTCs is reduced by removing one LTC at a time and re-assigning its assigned ranges to the other LTCs. This causes system throughput to drop back to 100,000 operations per second with 1 LTC.

## 5  Future Research Directions

Disaggregated database management systems are an emerging research topic that raise many interesting questions. For example, given a workload, what is an online framework to assemble a DBMS using microservices? What hardware and software co-designs maximize its efficiency? How does one verify the correctness of a composition? Is it possible for a system to learn patterns that maximize efficiency, enabling it to incorporate new hardware and services seamlessly? These and other research questions shape the future of disaggregated DBMSs.

**Acknowledgments.** We thank Liqid's Bob Brumfield and George Wagner for input on Sect. 2.2.

## References

1. Borthakur, D.: The aggregator leaf tailer architecture (2019). https://rockset.com/blog/aggregator-leaf-tailer-an-architecture-for-live-analytics-on-event-streams/
2. DeWitt, D.J., Ghandeharizadeh, S., Schneider, D.A., Bricker, A., Hsiao, H.I., Rasmussen, R.: The Gamma database machine project. In: IEEE Transactions on Knowledge and Data Engineering, vol. 1(2), March 1990
3. Dong, S., Callaghan, M., Galanis, L., Borthakur, D., Savor, T., Strum, M.: Optimizing space amplification in RocksDB. In: 8th Biennial Conference on Innovative Data Systems Research (CIDR 2017), Chaminade, CA (2017). https://www.cidrdb.org/

4. Gu, J., et al.: Efficient memory disaggregation with Infiniswap. In: 14th USENIX Symposium on Networked Systems Design and Implementation (NSDI 2017), pp. 649–667. USENIX Association, Boston, MA (2017)
5. Facebook: Multifeed (2015). https://engineering.fb.com/2015/03/10/production-engineering/serving-facebook-multifeed-efficiency-performance-gains-through-redesign/
6. Ghandeharizadeh, S., Huang, H., Nguyen, H.: Nova: diffused database processing using clouds of components [vision paper]. In: Kozielski, S., Mrozek, D., Kasprowski, P., Małysiak-Mrozek, B., Kostrzewa, D. (eds.) BDAS 2019. CCIS, vol. 1018, pp. 3–14. Springer, Cham (2019). https://doi.org/10.1007/978-3-030-19093-4_1
7. Ghandeharizadeh, S., Irani, S., Lam, J.: On configuring a hierarchy of storage media in the age of NVM. In: 2018 IEEE 34th International Conference on Data Engineering (ICDE), pp. 1380–1383. IEEE (2018)
8. Ghemawat, S., Dean, J.: LevelDB (2022). https://github.com/google/leveldb
9. Gupta, A.: Linkedin followfeed (2016). https://engineering.linkedin.com/blog/2016/03/followfeed-linkedin-s-feed-made-faster-and-smarter
10. Huang, H., Ghandeharizadeh, S.: An evaluation of RDMA-based message passing protocols. In: 2019 IEEE International Conference on Big Data, pp. 3854–3863. IEEE (2019)
11. Huang, H., Ghandeharizadeh, S.: Nova-LSM: a distributed, component-based LSM-tree key-value store. In: Proceedings of the 2021 International Conference on Management of Data, pp. 749–763 (2021)
12. Menon, J.: Next generation storage will be built with DPUs. Flash Memory Summit (2022)
13. Menon, J.: Next generation storage will use DPUs instead of CPUs. In: Storage Developer Conference (2022)
14. Noureddine, W.: The fungible DPU: a new category of microprocessor (2021). https://lp.fungible.com/hubfs/Assets/Whitepapers/The-Fungible-DPU-A-New-Category-of-Microprocessor.pdf
15. Executive Office of the President of the United States Machine Learning, Artificial Intelligence Subcommittee of the National Science, and Technology Council. Lessons Learned from Federal Use of Cloud Computing to Support Artificial Intelligence Research and Development (2022). https://www.whitehouse.gov/wp-content/uploads/2022/07/07-2022-Lessons-Learned-Cloud-for-AI-July2022.pdf
16. Rockset: Whitepaper (2022). https://rockset.com/whitepapers/rockset-concepts-designs-and-architecture/
17. Shan, Y., Huang, Y., Chen, Y., Zhang, Y.: LegoOS: a disseminated, distributed OS for hardware resource disaggregation. In: 13th USENIX Symposium on Operating Systems Design and Implementation (OSDI 2018), pp. 69–87 (2018)
18. Stonebraker, M.: The case for shared nothing. Database Engineering (1986)
19. Zhang, Q., Bernstein, P.A., Berger, D.S., Chandramouli, B.: Redy: remote dynamic memory cache. Proc. VLDB Endow. **15**(4), 766–779 (2021)
20. Zhang, Q., Bernstein, P.A., Berger, D.S., Chandramouli, B., Liu, V., Loo, B.T.: CompuCache: remote computable caching using spot VMs. In: Annual Conference on Innovative Data Systems Research (CIDR 2022) (2022)

# TPCx-AI on NVIDIA Jetsons

Robert Bayer$^{(\boxtimes)}$, Jon Voigt Tøttrup, and Pınar Tözün

IT University of Copenhagen, Copenhagen, Denmark
{roba,jvoi,pito}@itu.dk

**Abstract.** Despite their resource- and power-constrained nature, edge devices also exhibit an increase in the available compute and memory resources and heterogeneity, similar to the evolution of server hardware in the past decade. For example, NVIDIA Jetson devices have a system-on-chip (SoC) composed of an ARM CPU and an NVIDIA GPU sharing RAM that could be up to 32 GB. Such an SoC setup offers opportunities to push down complex computations closer to the data source rather than performing them on remote servers.

In this paper, we characterize the performance of two types of NVIDIA Jetson devices for end-to-end machine learning pipelines using the TPCx-AI benchmark. Our results demonstrate that the available memory is the main limitation to performance and scaling up machine learning workloads on edge devices. Despite this limitation, some edge devices show promise when comparing against a desktop hardware in terms of power-efficiency and reduction in data movement. In addition, exploiting the available compute parallelism on these devices can benefit not just model training and inference but also data pre-processing. By parallelizing, we get close to an *order of magnitude* improvement in pre-processing time for one of the TPCx-AI use cases. Finally, while TPCx-AI is a valuable benchmark, it is designed for server settings; therefore, the community needs an end-to-end machine learning benchmark targeting IoT/edge.

**Keywords:** TPCx-AI · system-on-chip · edge devices · IoT · performance benchmark · resource-aware · resource-constrained · machine learning

## 1 Introduction

In the past decade, we have seen major advances in the field of machine learning [1]. These advances have been mainly thanks to the availability of powerful hardware and large datasets. On the other hand, today, many data sources are actually small, low-powered edge or Internet-of-Things (IoT) devices, such as mobile phones, micro-controllers in sensors, wearable or self-driving smart platforms, etc. It becomes increasingly important to enable techniques that get more value out of data at these edge points rather than always sending the data to a remote and more powerful hardware device (such as a server in a data center) for further processing and training powerful machine learning models. Getting more value out of data closer to the source would be more secure, create new data-intensive applications at the edge, and enable more cost- and energy-efficient

R. Nambiar and M. Poess (Eds.): TPCTC 2022, LNCS 13860, pp. 49–66, 2023.
https://doi.org/10.1007/978-3-031-29576-8_4

use of data by reducing data movement. However, the challenge is operating on devices that are much more resource-constrained compared to the CPU-GPU co-processor servers that have sparked the machine learning advancements.

Parallel to the evolution of server hardware, the hardware resources available at the edge have also evolved. Such devices have already deployed System-on-Chip (SoC) designs that embraced hardware heterogeneity and co-processors earlier than server hardware. In addition, today, they come with increased memory and higher degree of compute parallelism. For example, NVIDIA offers Jetson devices for edge computing that have an SoC composed of an ARM CPU and an NVIDIA GPU sharing RAM that can be up to 32 GB depending on the device type. This evolution makes moving more data-intensive tasks closer to the sources of data more plausible.

This paper is a step toward understanding the capabilities and limitations of modern edge devices for machine learning pipelines. More specifically, we characterize the performance of two NVIDIA Jetson devices (TX2 and AGX Xavier) compared to a desktop hardware environment using the TPCx-AI standardized benchmark [2]. Both NVIDIA Jetson devices and TPCx-AI are relatively new and unexplored in our community. NVIDIA Jetson devices offer an interesting platform for machine learning at the edge, thanks to the available GPU and main memory. TPCx-AI offers an end-to-end perspective for machine learning, which allows testing the impact of different stages on resource-constrained hardware and the ability to scale the benchmark up and down, which enables stress-testing on devices offering varying compute and memory resources. While MLCommons [3] (formerly known as MLperf [4]) is the older and more mature standardized benchmark collection for machine learning and also offers benchmarks for edge devices and tiny hardware, it misses the end-to-end perspective and the workload scaling aspects of TPCx-AI. This study, therefore, also explores the new TPCx-AI benchmark and its potential when benchmarking modern edge devices. TPCx-IoT [5], which is the standardized TPC benchmark for IoT settings, neither targets AI nor would be easily extended for testing end-to-end machine learning.

The contributions of our performance characterization study is as follows:

1. Despite the increased memory resources at modern edge devices, our results show that the available memory is still the main limitation to performance and scaling up machine learning workloads on edge devices. Despite this limitation, a powerful edge device such as NVIDIA Jetson Xavier show potential to be competitive with a desktop hardware considering its power efficiency and omitted data movement costs.
2. We demonstrate that the increased hardware parallelism at the edge is an important asset that must be exploited. By implementing multi-threaded data pre-processing for one of the TPCx-AI uses cases, we get nearly an order of magnitude improvement in pre-processing time.
3. We find that even though TPCx-AI is an easy-to-deploy benchmark and can give valuable performance insights even on hardware platforms that it is not designed for, the community still needs an end-to-end machine learning benchmark targeting IoT/edge settings.

# 2 Background

This section describes what resource-aware machine learning constitutes and why it is important (Sect. 2.1), SoC architectures and their role in resource-aware machine learning (Sect. 2.2), and the TPCx-AI benchmark (Sect. 2.3).

## 2.1 Resource-Aware Machine Learning

Machine learning has become mainstream and is used in all industries, from product recommendation on the e-commerce platform [6] to X-ray classification in the medical industry [7]. The high predictive power of machine learning models, mainly deep learning models, comes at a price; the newer and better models have a higher computational cost [8] and, consequently, higher energy consumption.

While the accuracy of the trained models has traditionally been the primary metric of focus in machine learning, creating more transparency around the computational cost of models has gained traction recently [9–11]. This is also partially fueled by the higher focus on the climate crisis motivating researchers to be more resource-aware when designing new machine learning algorithms rather than always increasing hardware - and hence, energy consumption, to increase the model's predictive power. Resource-aware machine learning includes revised algorithms for more effective utilization of general-purpose or specialized hardware or designing specialized hardware for accelerating training and inference [12, 13]. The hardware focus here is not only the server hardware found in data centers but also more resource-constrained hardware found at *the edge*, representing the devices where data is captured such as handheld devices or sensors to collect data about the surroundings.

While the hardware resources on these devices are limited, the workloads are increasingly demanding, making efficiency even more critical. One solution to sidestep this problem is maintaining a steady connection between the data centers and edge devices so that sensor data can be processed quickly in the cloud. However, depending on the data size and proximity to the data center, this can take up too much bandwidth and incur high latency and energy costs. An alternate approach is to perform some or all computations involved in data processing at the place where the data is collected, *at the edge*. This is much more dependent on the capabilities of the device collecting the data, and in this work, our focus is to investigate these capabilities.

## 2.2 System-on-Chip Devices

System-on-chip (SoC) are devices that integrate all computer components into a single package. These can include CPU, I/O, RAM, and other specialized hardware, such as GPU, wireless radios, or programmable logic. SoCs have become popular with the rise of portable and edge devices and appear in laptops and desktop computers today.

The primary motivator for putting all of the electronics on a single chip is the energy consumption, which is reduced by increasing proximity of components, as energy consumption of data transfers is directly proportional to the distance of the transfer [14]. Furthermore, the higher energy efficiency correlates with thermal efficiency, where the heat dissipated from the SoC devices is much lower than their traditional counterparts. Lastly, the smaller size is also a very appealing feature, mainly for edge devices.

For CPU-GPU co-processors, an SoC design can share RAM between CPU and GPU. This eliminates costly memory transfers between CPU and GPU, leading to lower latency and energy consumption overall. Having memory shared also means that the total memory capacity can be increased, leading to previously unseen capacities for GPUs at the edge, which could alleviate the struggle data scientists meet when trying to train and deploy larger models.

### 2.3  TPCx-AI Benchmark

TPCx-AI [2] is a benchmark suite developed to test and evaluate the end-to-end machine learning capabilities of a system. The benchmark, which comes with a codebase, provides a platform that

- generates and processes large volumes of data mimicking real-world use cases,
- trains on pre-processed data to produce realistic machine learning models,
- conducts accurate insights for real-world customer scenarios based on the generated models,
- can scale to large-scale distributed configurations, and
- allows for flexibility in configuration changes to meet the demands of the dynamic AI landscape.

For the real-world use cases, the benchmark draws inspiration from the retail industry, where most companies utilize AI techniques to boost their competitiveness. The benchmark size is scalable to accommodate business needs of different sizes. Users can provide, amongst others, a scaling factor (SF), which indicates the size of the data set for benchmarking.

The benchmark consists of ten use cases, each taking advantage of a different machine learning techniques ranging from traditional techniques, such as k-means clustering and naive Bayes classifier, to more advanced and recent techniques, such as recurrent neural networks. The use cases incorporate diverse input data, where tabular data is complemented with image, audio, and textual data; and cover both supervised and unsupervised learning.

Out of the ten use cases only use cases 2, 5, and 9 rely on the use of a GPU. The rest of the use cases rely fully on the use of CPU. The distribution between the amount of data pre-processing and model training/serving varies across the use cases. Use cases 8, 9, and 10 are heavily skewed towards pre-processing. We especially focus on the pre-processing stage of use case 8 in Sect. 4.3.

**Test Phases.** One key distinguishing factor of TPCx-AI from the older MLCommons benchmark is its focus on end-to-end machine learning instead of solely focusing on training or inference. Therefore, the benchmark comprises six phases, described below, that run sequentially for each use case.

**(1) Load test (LT)** tests the process of copying the input files generated using the TPCx-AI data generator to the directories they will be fetched from during the benchmark run. This stage tests the storage infrastructure used during the benchmark run.

**(2) Power training test (PTT)** determines the maximum speed of training phase of each of the use cases, which includes the process to load and pre-process the data before the data is fed to the training process. It outputs (1) the total time of training in addition to the time taken per use case, and (2) the model files, which are to be used in the subsequent test phases.

**(3) & (4) Power serving test I & II (PST, PST1 & PST2)** determines the maximum speed at which the system-under-test can perform the serving phase of all use cases. Same as PTT, this test includes time to load and pre-process the data before the data is fed to the serving process.

**(5) Scoring test** performs a separate serving phase of each of the use cases on a newly generated dataset to determine the accuracy or error incurred by each of the use cases.

**(6) Throughput test (TT)** runs several concurrent streams, each containing all of the use cases in a unique order. This tests the ability of the system-under-test to serve models from different use cases to multiple users. The default value of the number of streams is 2, which can be modified.

**Metrics.** After every benchmark run, a report is computed by the benchmark utility, providing a set of metrics that can be used to compare the system-under-test with other systems.

The TPCx-AI benchmark defines their own set of metrics [2] [Benchmark Specification, Sect. 7.5].

$T_{ACRONYM}$ is the geometric mean of the time spent in seconds for each test phase per use case. *ACRONYM* corresponds to the acronym of the given test phase as listed above. For example, $T_{TT}$ means time spent in *throughput test* phase of the benchmark.

**AIUCpm@SF** is **AI U**se **C**ase **p**erformance **m**etric **at S**caling **F**actor and summarizes a subset of the other performance metrics in a single scalar value. It is computed by the following formula, where $SF$ is the scaling factor and $N$ is the number of use cases (always 10):

$$\frac{SF \cdot N \cdot 60}{\sqrt[4]{T_{LT} \cdot T_{PTT} \cdot T_{PST} \cdot T_{TT}}}$$

**DATAGEN** is the time spent in seconds generating the complete data-set.

**$/AIUCpm@SF** is a metric to highlight price per performance. For Transaction Processing and Performance Council (TPC), it is customary to report the total cost of a system divided by the achieved performance [15]. This is also a useful metric that gives a rough estimate of how much value for money that a system yields. In our experiments, the performance metric is AIUCpm@SF and the currency is USD.

Except for $AIUCpm@SF$, lower values are better for these metrics.

## 3   Related Work

TPCx-AI is a relatively new standardized benchmark [16]. Hence, to the best of our knowledge, our work is the first study that utilizes TPCx-AI for performance characterization of hardware, especially edge devices, since the introduction of TPCx-AI in [17].

In contrast, several works have tested edge devices for artificial intelligence. In [18], an NVIDIA Jetson Nano, a Raspberry Pi 4, a Google Coral Dev Board and an Arduino Nano 33 BLE microcontroller are benchmarked on selected deep learning tasks focusing on training and inference. In [19], a benchmark suite is developed targeting machine learning and cognitive science applications to test cloud, edge, and mobile devices. The benchmark is also adapted to test distributed computers serving multiple end-users. In addition to working on benchmarks, in [20], the authors focus on model instability at the edge.

Our work is complementary to these works since our aim is to study the performance of modern powerful edge devices such as NVIDIA Jetsons for end-to-end machine learning tasks (not just inference or training). In parallel, we are investigating the potential of the TPCx-AI benchmark beyond benchmarking on server hardware.

## 4   Experimental Methodology and Setup

Our goal is to characterize the performance of modern, powerful edge devices for end-to-end machine learning. This section presents the experimental methodology and setup we deploy to achieve this goal.

### 4.1   Systems

To represent state-of-the-art modern edge devices, we pick two offerings from NVIDIA with varying hardware resources. In addition, we use a desktop hardware setup as the baseline to compare against the edge devices. Section 4.1 summarizes the specifications of these devices.

**NVIDIA Jetson TX2**, labeled TX2 in short, is a portable SoC composed of a power-efficient ARM-CPU & NVIDIA GPU, designed for embedded systems that require GPU-friendly computations, e.g., image processing, video encoding/decoding, and machine learning tasks. TX2 used in our experiments comes with 8 GB RAM (shared between CPU & GPU) and 32 GB eMMC storage, a 6-core $\sim$ 2 GHz ARM64 CPU and 256 CUDA Core GPU [21,22]. The device can operate at a wattage between 7.5 W–15 W. We configured our TX2 to operate at 15 W, increasing the maximum clock rates but doubling power consumption.

We also added extra storage in the form of an SD-card (32 GB) to fit the entire TPCx-AI benchmark suite.

To accommodate the memory requirements of TPCx-AI scaling factors 1-3, we reserved 12 GB of disk space as swap memory, in addition to the default of ~ 4 GB compressed swap memory (`zram`).

**NVIDIA Jetson AGX Xavier**, labeled `Xavier` in short, is also a portable computer by NVIDIA, but with more powerful hardware and designed specifically for autonomous machines [23]. Xavier used in our experiments has an 8-core ~ 2.2 GHz ARM64 CPU, a 512 CUDA-core GPU and ~ 32 GB memory shared between the CPU and GPU. The device can operate at a wattage between 15 W–30 W. As with TX2, we configured the device to operate at the maximum wattage (30 W) to maximize clock rates despite the double power consumption. Like TX2, the device is fitted with 32 GB eMMC storage [21], but unlike TX2, we opted to add a USB 3.0 storage device (64 GB).

Software-wise, both TX2 and Xavier runs NVIDIA's Ubuntu distribution for the Jetsons, as provided by NVIDIA Jetpack [24] on both devices. We also used Jetpack to install the most commonly used machine learning libraries such as CUDnn and OpenCV.

**Desktop** setup, also labeled as `Desktop`, that we used as a baseline for our comparisons includes an NVIDIA GeForce RTX 2070 GPU and an x86 6th gen Intel i7 CPU with 16 GiB RAM. The power consumption of the device is estimated from the power requirements of the GPU to be at most 550 W [25].

As a rule of thumb, the power consumption can be assumed to be about one order of magnitude above that of a Jetson device.

**Table 1.** Systems-under-test in our experiments. The information for the Jetson devices are taken from [21, 26]. The *price* column represents manufacturer suggested retail price, which we couldn't find for all the Desktop components.

| Device | GPU | CPU | RAM | PWR | Price |
|---|---|---|---|---|---|
| TX2 | NVIDIA Pascal, 256 CUDA Cores | NVIDIA Denver (2 Cores) & Arm Cortex A57 (4 Cores) @ 2.0 GHz | 8 GB | 15 W | $399 |
| Xavier | NVIDIA Volta, 512 CUDA Cores, 64 Tensor Cores | 8 Cores ARM v8.2 64-bit @ 2.2 GHz | 32 GB | 30 W | $699 |
| Desktop | NVIDIA RTX 2070, 2304 CUDA Cores, 288 Tensor Cores | 8 Cores Intel Core i7-6700K @ 4.0 GHz | 16 GB (CPU), 8 GB (GPU) | ~ 550 W | – |

## 4.2   Metrics

The metrics used to reason about the performance of Jetsons is organized into three categories: application-level (reported by TPCx-AI), hardware utilization, and power consumption metrics.

**Application-Level.** These are the metrics reported by TPCx-AI (see Sect. 2.3). We omit the DATAGEN metric due to the added network overhead overshadowing the actual data generation time in our setup (see Section 4.3).

**Hardware Utilization.** While the benchmark metrics show how quickly the system completes different AI-related tasks, it leaves the question of how *efficiently* the resources of this system are utilized while performing these tasks. Understanding hardware utilization characteristics can also help comprehend performance differences across the benchmark use cases and hardware systems.

To measure hardware utilization, we monitor the CPU and GPU utilization and memory consumption, at each second using the tegrastats utility provided by NVIDIA for Tegra-chipset [27], which is what the Jetson devices have. On the desktop hardware, we use nvidia-smi [28] and ps [29] utility provided by NVIDIA and unix, respectively, for the same measurements.

**Power Consumption.** In addition to the hardware utilization, we record the power consumption of each device to explore efficiency further. For the NVIDIA Jetson devices, the system power consumption is collected by the tegrastats utility. However, there is no way to collect the complete information through the available software for the desktop. In that case, we only collect the GPU's power consumption reported by nvidia-smi. The power consumption is recorded as a snapshot measurement of system wattage in both cases. To complement this, we accumulate the power consumption over time as a single watt-hour measurement for each use case of each benchmark run.

## 4.3   Benchmark Suite Modifications

We made three modifications to the TPCx-AI benchmark suite[1]: (1) to run the benchmarks in a non-x86 environment, (2) bug fix related to the batch size in Use Case 5, and (3) a performance-related modification.

First, the data-generation component of the TPCx-AI benchmark suite (the PDGF[2, Specification p. 64]) is compiled for x86-64 architectures only and cannot run on our Jetson devices. Therefore, we set up a separate Intel x86-64 machine with a purpose-built HTTP server to run the data-generation software and provide the generated data files. On our Jetson devices, we replaced the PDGF-executable with an executable that acts as a client for the HTTP server. This way, we move the data from the x86 machine to the Jetsons over the network before the benchmarking phase starts.

---

[1] The changes we made to the codebase can be found at https://github.com/ContainedBlargh/TPCx-AI-on-Nvidia-Jetsons.

Then, we discovered a bug in Use Case 5 (line 166), where a parameter `batch` was not being passed to the `serve` function, leading to much higher memory demands for serving than for training. As that parameter is configurable but not passed, we assumed this was a bug.

Finally, we changed the data pre-processing step of Use Case 8 to be multi-threaded, which improved the times to run this use case drastically. In Section 5.3, we highlight the performance impact of this modification.

# 5 Results

We ran the TPCx-AI benchmark five times and reported the mean and standard deviation for each configuration (device & scaling factor). As for the scaling factor, we use the values of 1 and 3, as higher scaling factors cannot fit in Jetson devices. Unless stated otherwise using the label `original`, all reported results are with the modified version of use case 8. The results are split into three parts: (1) overall results from the whole benchmark run, (2) time-breakdowns for each use case, and (3) impact of parallelizing pre-processing of use case 8.

**Table 2.** TPCx-AI metrics (see Sect. 2.3 for details). *Due to unknown price, the $/AIUCpm@SF has been omitted.

| Metric | | TX2, SF = 1 | Xavier, SF = 1 | Xavier, SF = 3 | Desktop, SF = 1 | Desktop, SF = 3 |
|---|---|---|---|---|---|---|
| AIUCpm@SF | Mean | 8.18 | 28.91 | 31.10 | 90.15 | 152.29 |
| | St. dev. | 2.54 | 1.48 | 3.80 | 2.42 | 5.19 |
| $/AIUCpm@SF | Mean | 37.84 | 24.23 | 22.73 | –* | –* |
| | St. dev | 9.10 | 1.29 | 2.66 | –* | –* |
| $T_{LT}$ (seconds) | Mean | 39.34 s | 1.85 s | 27.72 s | 1.33 s | 2.33 s |
| | St. dev. | 19.81 s | 0.40 s | 13.57 s | 0.04 s | 0.25 s |
| $T_{PTT}$ (seconds) | Mean | 308.19 s | 94.66 s | 198.88 s | 34.91 s | 84.17 s |
| | St. dev. | 7.10 s | 3.27 s | 5.66 s | 1.45 s | 3.53 s |
| $T_{PST}$ (seconds) | Mean | 48.51 s | 28.06 s | 45.49 s | 6.99 s | 10.28 s |
| | St. dev. | 1.42 s | 0.67 s | 2.19 s | 0.38 s | 0.09 s |
| $T_{TT}$ (seconds) | Mean | 72.89 s | 38.52 s | 50.91 s | 6.06 s | 9.75 s |
| | St. dev. | 4.10 s | 1.65 s | 3.12 s | 0.34 s | 0.13 s |

## 5.1 Whole Benchmark Run

Table 2 lists the mean and standard deviation values for the metrics reported by TPCx-AI. To help us explain some of these benchmark metrics, Table 3 presents

**Table 3.** Total memory (MB) swapped to disk during training of all use cases.

| Total swapped | TX2, SF = 1, original | TX2, SF = 1 | Xavier, SF = 1 | Xavier, SF = 3 | Desktop, SF = 1 | Desktop, SF = 3 |
|---|---|---|---|---|---|---|
| Mean (MB) | 4271.8 | 3974.6 | 0.30 | 1008.99 | 3597.33 | 19335.2 |

the amount of memory swapped during the whole benchmark run for each device. When we monitored the hardware utilization information throughout the benchmark runs, it became clear that memory was the primary resource under pressure. All the hardware devices used in this work have relatively limited physical memory (8 GB to 32 GB) compared to today's state-of-the-art server hardware in data centers (100 GB to TBs). As a result, when the working dataset size of TPCx-AI does not fit into the available device memory, it triggers *memory swaps*, meaning parts of the working memory are moved to the disk so that currently required data can be loaded into memory. Thus, instead of showing CPU/GPU utilization, we have results for swapped memory here.

Looking at the benchmark's performance summary metric, *AIUCpm*, Desktop hardware is an order of magnitude better than TX2. As Table 3 demonstrates, TX2 exhibits a high number of swaps due to its smaller memory size, which results in this behavior. In addition, the SD card in TX2 causes a high $T_{LT}$, which is the most data-intensive task, since it includes reading/writing data from persistent storage.

Comparing Xavier to Desktop hardware, the difference in performance increases with a higher scaling factor. However, Xavier performs roughly the same in terms of *AIUCpm* across the two scaling factors showing that it scales well with the increase in scaling factor. In addition, it has larger main memory and exhibits the lowest number of swaps. However, it has two main bottlenecks compared to Desktop, which results in lower performance. First, Xavier has a slower ARM processor compared to the x86 in Desktop. Second, the eMMC-based storage is also slower than the SATA SSD in Desktop, as highlighted by the different behavior between the $T_{LT}$ results for the two scaling factors.

We leave the parameters that determine the degree of parallelism to default values set by TPCx-AI, except for the pre-processing phase of use case 8 (see Sect. 5.3). Looking at the results for $T_{PTT}$, $T_{PST}$, $T_{TT}$, we see the impact of both the differences in processor speed and the different degrees of hardware parallelism each device provides.

From a price/performance perspective, *$/AIUCPm*, both Jetson devices perform similarly.

Lastly, Table 4 presents the total power consumption for each device for the whole benchmark run. Despite the lower power draw of TX2 compared to the other devices (Sect. 4.1), it consumes the highest power to complete the benchmark since it takes a longer time to complete a benchmark run. Xavier behaves similarly to Desktop even though the Desktop results only count the GPU power

**Table 4.** Total power consumption by device across all benchmarks in watt-hours. Note that **Desktop** power measurements are GPU-only.

| Power consumption | TX2, SF = 1, original | TX2, SF = 1 | Xavier, SF = 1 | Xavier, SF = 3 | Desktop, SF = 1 | Desktop, SF = 3 |
|---|---|---|---|---|---|---|
| Mean (Wh) | 30.31 | 19.09 | 8.24 | 16.27 | 10.23 | 12.50 |
| St. dev (Wh) | 0.58 | 0.34 | 0.21 | 0.78 | 1.21 | 0.32 |

consumption. Based on this, **Xavier** is competitive in terms of power/performance ratio over the other devices.

## 5.2  Time-Breakdown per Use Case

Figure 1 and Fig. 2 breaks the training (Phase #2) and serving (Phase #3 & #4) phase (Sect. 2.3) of each use case in the benchmark, respectively. TPCx-AI reports time ($T_{PTT}$ and $T_{PST}$) at a coarse granularity from these phases for the individual use cases. We further break this time into *loading*, which is the time to fetch data from storage and join/merge them if there are multiple data files, *pre-processing*, which is the time to pre-process the data to be fed to training/serving, and *training/serving*, which is the time that goes to actual training/serving.

The figures show that **TX2** takes the most time and **Desktop** hardware takes the least time to complete the phases. This is expected considering the hardware resources available on these devices and the results reported in Sect. 5.1. Furthermore, we observe that different use cases stress the different phases of training and serving. Use case 1 exhibits higher loading times, while training/serving times dominate the time-breakdown for use cases 2, 4, 5, 6, and 7. On the other hand, for use cases 8, 9, and 10, the pre-processing times are more pronounced (as also Sect. 2.3 highlights). This shows that TPCx-AI use cases exhibit a good variety in terms of the machine learning tasks they stress at runtime.

Comparing the results of scaling factors (SF) 1 and 3, there is no direct scaling of runtimes for different components. For some use cases, the times roughly triple, but in most cases, they are sub- or super-scalar. We omit SF=3 results for **TX2** due to its prohibitively long run times, which are a result of the low memory (8 GB) on this device causing frequent swap operations (Table 3).

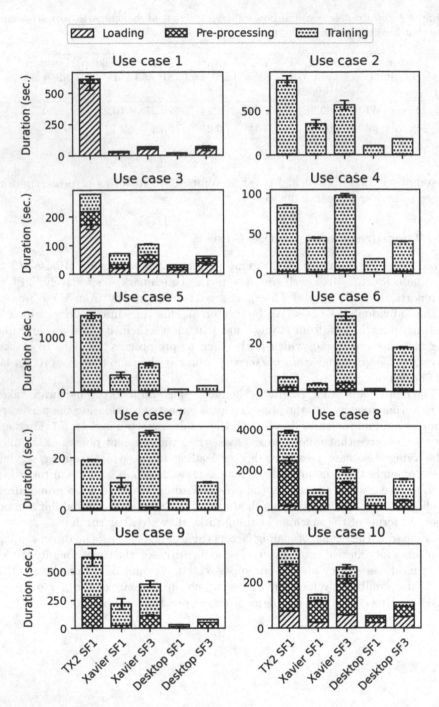

**Fig. 1.** Time-breakdown of the training phase of individual TPCx-AI use cases using revised use case 8. Notice the different scale on y-axes.

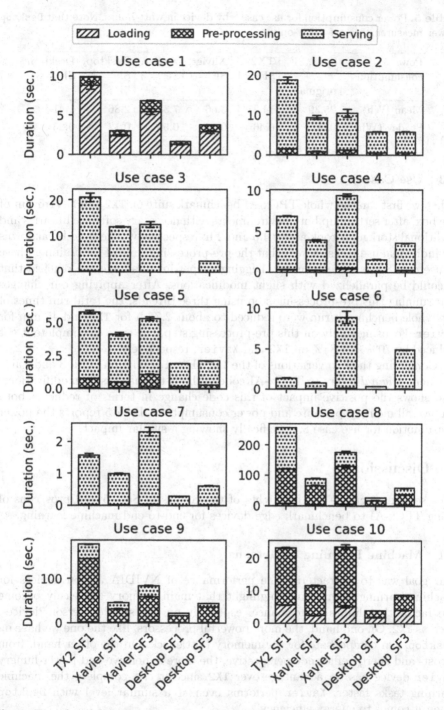

**Fig. 2.** Time-breakdown of the serving phase of individual TPCx-AI use cases using revised use case 8. Notice the different scale on y-axes.

**Table 5.** Power consumption for use case 8 by device in watt-hours. Note that `Desktop` power measurements are GPU-only.

| Power consumption | TX2, SF = 1, original | TX2, SF = 1 | Xavier, SF = 1 | Xavier, SF = 3 | Desktop, SF = 1 | Desktop, SF = 3 |
|---|---|---|---|---|---|---|
| Mean (Wh) | 25.39 | 14.27 | 3.66 | 7.38 | 2.86 | 1.41 |
| St. dev (Wh) | 0.50 | 0.46 | 0.10 | 0.56 | 0.12 | 0.25 |

### 5.3    Use Case 8

When we first ran the whole TPCx-AI benchmark suite on `TX2` and `Xavier` out of the box, after setting up both environments with necessary software libraries and additional storage, it took about 4.5 and 2 h, respectively. The time-breakdowns for individual use cases showed that the pre-processing time of the training phase of use case 8 was a clear outlier. Digging deeper into its code, we realized that it could be parallelized with slight modifications. After applying our changes and running this pre-processing step using three threads, the total run times of the whole benchmark run were reduced to about 2.75 h for `TX2` and 45 min for `Xavier`. Focusing solely on this pre-processing step, the time to complete it got reduced by 70% and 84% on `TX2` and `Xavier`, respectively.

Comparing the two variations of the `TX2` SF = 1 results on Table 3 and Table 4, where *original* refers to TPCx-AI code without the use case 8 modifications, also shows the positive impact of this code change in terms of reducing both the overall memory pressure and power consumption. Table 5 reports the power consumption for use case 8, specifically showing a similar impact.

## 6    Discussion

This section discusses the highlights of the results in Sect. 5 and pros/cons of using TPCx-AI to benchmark edge devices for end-to-end machine learning.

### 6.1    Machine Learning on Jetsons

Our goal was to characterize the performance of NVIDIA Jetson devices for machine learning. Our results highlight that main memory can easily become the factor that limits performance, especially on the smaller Jetson devices, such as `TX2`. On one hand, the more powerful processors, like the one we have on `Desktop`, can compensate for the memory bottleneck. On the other hand, from a cost- and energy-efficiency perspective, the more expensive and power-hungry `Xavier` device has an advantage over `TX2` since it can complete the machine learning tasks faster. `Xavier` performs even at a similar level with `Desktop` when it comes to energy-efficiency.

In a data center setting, it is common wisdom [30] that if an application is latency-critical, a fast multicore x86 processor, like the one on `Desktop`, is more performance-efficient than an ARM processor, like the one on Xavier and TX2. Our results also corroborate this wisdom if we assume that all the processing is done locally omitting the cost of going over the network. More specifically, the Jetson devices are designed for the edge. In addition to being designed for energy-efficiency, they are also deployed at the source of data collection. In contrast, Desktop would be a device where the data is sent to for further processing from its source device. Therefore, when considering latency in an edge setting, one must take into account the cost of moving the data from the source to another device if the processing cannot be done at the edge. From this perspective, declaring a clear winner between Xavier and Desktop for latency is challenging.

## 6.2    TPCx-AI Benchmark for Edge Devices

TPCx-AI is a relatively new standardized benchmark and has not been designed with edge/IoT settings in mind. It targets end-to-end machine learning at data center or high-performance computing settings, where both compute and memory resources are plenty. Such settings can handle the memory pressure and throughput needs of TPCx-AI easily. In addition, the reference TPCx-AI implementation, while tremendously helpful for using the benchmark almost out of the box, is there to guide people to deploy the same use cases on the machine learning framework they want to analyze.

In our work, we use TPCx-AI on edge devices, which are designed to minimize latency at small-scale rather than throughput, i.e., work quickly with small-scale data, and to be energy-efficient. We also aimed at using TPCx-AI's reference implementation as is. One can claim that our setup is not an ideal use of this benchmark. However, for testing end-to-end machine learning, to the best of our knowledge, there is no other viable option. In addition, the ability to scale the workloads up and down using scaling factors, which is a common functionality in TPC benchmarks, is very valuable for testing hardware with differing resource characteristics. Thus, testing the potential of this benchmark at the edge settings was worthwhile to us.

Overall, we found that using the python-based reference implementation; one can use TPCx-AI *almost* out of the box, even for edge settings. The main challenge against using it directly out of the box was the data generation component, which is closed source and built for x86 environments. Thus, we had to generate our data on an x86 machine and move our data to the edge device (Sect. 4.3). For the python libraries, using the counter-parts available on the Jetson was relatively straightforward. While all this still requires non-negligible setup time, it was feasible since it took us a couple weeks, not months.

On the other hand, even the TPCx-AI scale factor 1 is too big for the memory resources of the smallest device we had, TX2. In addition, the nature of the throughput tests where multiple models were in use may not be representative for edge settings where typically a few models would be deployed. Furthermore, considering the higher availability of CPU parallelism and GPU resources at the edge, having more parts of the reference implementation that can exploit CPU parallelism or run on a GPU would be helpful. Finally, when testing hardware, especially at the edge, both cost- and power-efficiency must be considered in addition to the *AIUCpm*. Although TPC also has a standardized way to measure power/performance trade-off, it is rarely reported in the results published on TPC's webpage. Considering our results and increasing importance of being power-efficient, we argue that more people should publish power results.

Going forward, when designing an end-to-end machine learning benchmark, it is preferable if the reference implementation can scale the workload up and down similar to TPCx-AI but simultaneously have the ability to scale the datasets further down and exploit more and different types of hardware parallelism. While doing this design, the use cases and throughput tests should be adjusted accordingly. For example, one can include a *transfer learning* (partial training on pre-trained models) use case since edge devices today are rarely used for the full training of the models. On the other hand, having a few full training cases would be interesting to observe the strengths of a particular device.

Lastly, one can also devise an experimental study by picking and choosing different combinations of use cases instead of running the full benchmark suite. While this was possible for TPCx-AI, we have not investigated this route yet.

## 7    Conclusion

In this work, we performed a performance characterization study of two modern high-end edge devices, NVIDIA Jetson TX2 and AGX Xavier, for end-to-end machine learning. We identified the TPCx-AI benchmark as a good candidate for generating the workload for such a study and a consume-grade CPU-GPU co-processor, desktop machine, as a baseline. Our study shows that the small memory of TX2 is a limiting factor of performance, while Xavier achieves a good cost- and energy-efficiency. In addition, exploiting the increasing degrees and types of hardware parallelism is not only crucial for big server settings but also for the edge. Finally, while TPCx-AI provided us with many valuable insights without high deployment cost, a more thorough characterization of such edge devices requires a benchmark that is specialized for end-to-end machine learning for the edge/IoT settings.

**Acknowledgements.** The work is funded by the Independent Research Fund Denmark's (Danmarks Frie Forskningsfond; DFF) Inge Lehmann program under grant agreement number 0171-00062B and the European Union's Horizon 2020 research and innovation program under grant agreement number 957407. We further thank DASYA lab members at IT University of Copenhagen for their support.

# References

1. Krizhevsky, A., Sutskever, I., Hinton, G.E.: ImageNet classification with deep convolutional neural networks. In: NIPS, pp. 1097–1105 (2012)
2. Transaction Processing Performance Council (TPC). TPC Express AI (TPCx-AI) Standard Specification Revision 1.0.0
3. MLCommons. https://mlcommons.org/en/
4. Mattson, P., Cheng, C., Diamos, G., et al.: MLPerf training benchmark. In: MLSys, pp. 336–349 (2020)
5. Transaction Processing Performance Council (TPC). TPC Express IoT (TPCx-IoT) Standard Specification Revision 2.0.1
6. Wang, J., Huang, P., Zhao, H., Zhang, Z., Zhao, B., Lee, D.L.: Billion-scale commodity embedding for e-commerce recommendation in Alibaba (2018)
7. Kermany, D.S., Goldbaum, M., Cai, W., et al.: Identifying medical diagnoses and treatable diseases by image-based deep learning. Cell **172**(5), 1122–1131 (2018)
8. OpenAI. AI and Compute (2018). https://openai.com/blog/ai-and-compute/ Accessed 31 Mar 2022
9. Strubell, E., Ganesh, A., McCallum, A.: Energy and policy considerations for deep learning in NLP. In: ACL, pp. 3645–3650 (2019)
10. Schwartz, R., Dodge, J., Smith, N.A., Etzioni, O.: Green AI. CACM **63**(12), 54–63 (2020)
11. Patterson, D., Gonzalez, J., Le, Q., et al.: Carbon emissions and large neural network training (2021)
12. Chen, Y.-H., Krishna, T., Emer, J.S., Sze, V.: Eyeriss: an energy efficient reconfigurable accelerator for deep convolutional neural networks. IEEE J. Solid-State Circuits **52**(1), 127–138 (2017)
13. Yang, T.-J., Chen, Y.-H., Sze, V.: Designing energy-efficient convolutional neural networks using energy-aware pruning. In: CVPR (2017)
14. Adhinarayanan, V., Paul, I., Greathouse, J.L., Huang, W., Pattnaik, A., Feng, W.-C.: Measuring and modeling on-chip interconnect power on real hardware. In: IISWC, pp. 1–11 (2016)
15. Transaction Processing and Performance Council. TPC Express Benchmark™ AI - Full Disclosure Report (2022)
16. Ihde, N., et al.: A survey of big data, high performance computing, and machine learning benchmarks. In: Nambiar, R., Poess, M. (eds.) TPCTC 2021. LNCS, vol. 13169, pp. 98–118. Springer, Cham (2022). https://doi.org/10.1007/978-3-030-94437-7_7
17. Rabl, T., et al.: ADABench - towards an industry standard benchmark for advanced analytics. In: Nambiar, R., Poess, M. (eds.) TPCTC 2019. LNCS, vol. 12257, pp. 47–63. Springer, Cham (2020). https://doi.org/10.1007/978-3-030-55024-0_4
18. Baller, S.P., Jindal, A., Chadha, M., Gerndt, M.: DeepEdgeBench: benchmarking deep neural networks on edge devices, pp. 20–30 (2021)
19. Hao, T., Hwang, K., Zhan, J., Li, Y., Cao, Y.: Scenario-based AI benchmark evaluation of distributed cloud/edge computing systems. In: IEEE ToCs, p. 1 (2022)
20. Cidon, E., Pergament, E., Asgar, Z., Cidon, A., Katti, S.: Characterizing and taming model instability across edge devices. In: MLSys, pp. 624–636
21. NVIDIA. Jetson Modules (2021). https://developer.nvidia.com/embedded/jetson-modules. Accessed 10 Feb 2022
22. NVIDIA. Jetson TX2 Module (2021). https://developer.nvidia.com/embedded/jetson-tx2. Accessed 10 Feb 2022

23. NVIDIA. Jetson AGX Xavier Modules (2021). https://developer.nvidia.com/embedded/jetson-agx-xavier. Accessed 10 Feb 2022
24. NVIDIA. JetPack SDK (2021). https://developer.nvidia.com/embedded/jetpack. Accessed 10 Feb 2022
25. NVIDIA. RTX 2070 (2022). https://www.nvidia.com/en-me/geforce/graphicscards/rtx-2070/. Accessed 28 Feb 2022
26. NVIDIA. Jetson FAQ—NVIDIA Developer (2021). https://developer.nvidia.com/embedded/faq#jetson-prices. Accessed 31 May 2022
27. NVIDIA. Tegrastats Utility (2021). https://docs.nvidia.com/drive/drive_os_5.1.6.1L/nvvib_docs/index.html#page/DRIVE_OS_Linux_SDK_Development_Guide/Utilities/util_tegrastats.html. Accessed 23 Feb 2022
28. pmav99. Nvsmi (2022). https://github.com/pmav99/nvsmi. Accessed 03 Mar 2022
29. Rodola, G.: Psutil (2022). https://github.com/giampaolo/psutil. Accessed 03 Mar 2022
30. Hölzle, U.: Brawny cores still beat wimpy cores, most of the time. In: IEEE Micro, pp. 23–24 (2010)

# More the Merrier: Comparative Evaluation of TPCx-AI and MLPerf Benchmarks for AI

Yingrui Liu Olesiuk, Miro Hodak, David Ellison, and Ajay Dholakia[✉]

Lenovo, Infrastructure Solutions Group, Morrisville, NC, USA
{Yolesiuk,dellison,adholakia}@lenovo.com, Miro.Hodak@amd.com

**Abstract.** With AI systems and solutions increasingly being deployed across many industries, measuring performance of AI workloads remains a priority in computing. TPCx-AI is a new benchmarking suite developed by TPC to address this need. It provides an alternative to MLPerf benchmarking suite that has already been adopted by many of the main players in AI. This paper compares the two benchmarks and shows pros and cons of each. We explain that the two approaches differ in scope, with TPCx-AI attempting to capture end-to-end AI process while MLPerf focuses only on the most computationally heavy AI tasks: Training and Inference. Another significant difference is scoring with TPCx-AI using a single number, while MLPerf using many scores to represent performance at a more granular level. We also present our experience with both suites and offer recommendation when to use each tool.

**Keywords:** Artificial Intelligence · Inference · Training · MLPerf · TPCx-AI · Deep Learning · Performance

## 1 Introduction

The release of TPCx-AI [1, 2] in August 2021 was an important step in benchmarking AI workloads, as it comes from a well-respected organization promoting fair measurement of different computational workloads. The new tool joins an already crowded field of AI benchmarking tools. MLPerf, created by the MLCommons organization, is a leader in this area, having a sizeable community of technological leaders in AI space and regular releases with dozens of submitters.

While there are many AI benchmarking tools available, they differ in which part of the AI workload they focus on. Because "AI workload" does not have a fixed definition and is often implemented differently, the available tools measure different parts of the workloads and/or define the workloads in different ways. In that sense, none of the existing tools can be said to measure the same thing as each one measures the AI process differently. Consequently, the results are not directly comparable and when applied on the same type of HW, the competitive ranking can be different.

AI benchmarking tools can be divided according to the tasks they cover in the AI process. At the one end of the spectrum are micro-benchmarks that measure performance of individual computational operations important for AI. Another level is measuring

© The Author(s), under exclusive license to Springer Nature Switzerland AG 2023
R. Nambiar and M. Poess (Eds.): TPCTC 2022, LNCS 13860, pp. 67–77, 2023.
https://doi.org/10.1007/978-3-031-29576-8_5

certain important steps in AI workloads, such as Training or Inference. MLPerf is an example of this approach. Finally, some tools attempt to evaluate the whole end-to-end AI workload, including data generation, cleaning, training, inference, etc. TPCx-AI takes this approach. Broadly speaking, the earliest AI benchmarking tools tend to focus on micro-benchmarking, while more recent ones take a more holistic approach to the AI performance measurement.

The goal of this work is to examine and compare MLPerf and TPCx-AI as tools for measuring AI performance and find under which scenario is one preferable to the other. As a long time MLPerf submitters, we evaluate the TPCx-AI as a new tool and examine if it brings appreciable improvements for submitters and/or customers wanting to purchase AI systems. We have previously published a few studies [3, 4] evaluating MLPerf as an AI benchmarking tool pointing out its strengths and weaknesses and this work builds on that and includes TPCx-AI as a new entry in the field.

A key contribution of this paper is the first side-by-side evaluation of two of the leading AI benchmarks, delving into details of each and illustrating areas where they differ from each other. Another key contribution is an analysis of the performance metric used in TPCx-AI benchmark and an alternative computation that enables a more representative metric value.

This paper is organized as follows: Sect. 2 gives overview of the field of AI benchmarking, Sect. 3 describes MLPerf benchmarks, Sect. 4 gives an overview of TPCx-AI. Section 5 compares the two benchmarking suites and Sect. 6 gives Summary and Conclusions.

## 2   AI Benchmarking Tools

AI benchmarking work in industry as well as academia has been ramping up over the past few years. While performance evaluation of AI workloads has been an active area of research, benchmark development has been a more recent trend. A survey of such recent benchmarking initiatives and evaluation of associated requirements from metrics and system parameters is given in [5]. Initial attempts focused on deep learning model training for computationally intensive tasks like image classification. DeepBench [6] from Baidu Research was one of the early projects and targeted low-level operations such as matrix multiplications and convolutions that are key parts of deep learning algorithms. The goal of DeepBench was to characterize hardware designs best suited for these low-level operations, including communication tasks. Latest published results are from 2019.

Another project, DAWNBench [7], led by Stanford University, aimed to evaluate end-to-end deep learning including training and inference stages. The inclusion of AI inference alongside model training in the benchmark scope was driven by the need to address the end-user adoption of AI in the form of using trained models for prediction and other inference scenarios. The project was eventually abandoned for MLPerf.

AIPerf [8] is a recent benchmark proposal aimed at combined AI-HPC usage scenarios. The convergence of AI and HPC systems has created a complex system stack combining AI software frameworks with powerful HPC computing systems. AIPerf aims to benchmark use of such systems for running real practical problems as opposed to fixed workloads. It uses automated machine learning (AutoML) as workload that scales, proposes the operation rate of neural networks as a metric that is evaluated to assess scalability and stability of the benchmark. The use of AutoML addresses the concerns about HPC computations being FP-64 while most AI applications requiring FP-32 or even FP16 computations.

HPL-AI [9] is a mixed-precision benchmark that adapts the HPC staple LINPACK benchmark to meet AI needs. It enables HPC experts to quickly estimate AI capabilities of their systems.

MLPerf [10–12] has emerged as the most popular AI benchmark initiative over the past four years. MLPerf expanded the scope of benchmarking outcome by defining more metrics for a benchmark run to collect and report. Furthermore, the list of tasks included in the benchmark has also been expanded. Starting with a group of enterprises lead by Google, NVIDIA and Intel, the roster of participants has steadily grown. MLPerf appears to be ahead of traditional benchmarking organizations in formulating usable benchmark specifications. The ever-growing interest in AI, with its associated complexity, ongoing active research and a shortage of talent to meet the demands are all contributing factors.

Finally, TPCx-AI [1] has been released one year ago to enable end-to-end benchmarking of AI workflows, from data sourcing to deploying or serving trained models in production. This perspective for benchmarking AI systems is in contrast with other benchmarks that focus on specific steps like training and inference.

## 3 MLPerf AI Benchmarks

MLPerf is an AI benchmarking suite that was first released in 2018, when the first iteration of its AI Training suite was released. It was denoted 0.5, since then 5 more rounds have been published, most recent in June 2022, version 2.0. Inference suite debuted in 2019 with version 2019 and 4 more versions has been published since, most recent one in April 2022, labeled as 2.0. Over time, the release cadence settled to 2 rounds for both Training and Inference, respectively, in a year.

To publish an MLPerf result, an organization has to submit at a date prescribed by MLPerf schedule for a given version of the benchmark. This is followed by several weeks of peer reviews, at which point results get posted online. That is, there are no rolling submissions as is the case with some of the other industry benchmarks. Each category, i.e., Training and Inference, has a working group that works on updating the benchmarks to keep them up-to-date with the state of the art in the industry. Prior to a submission deadline, specifications along with a reference code is released. For submissions, the reference code is re-implemented for particular hardware architectures – this is usually done by chip manufacturers and has to follow strict rules to be considered equivalent. The optimized code is what is used for submissions – the reference code is, usually, several times slower. In general, there are 3 classes of submitters: Chip manufacturers, cloud provider, and server OEMs.

MLPerf is governed by MLCommons organization created in 2020, which has many of the AI leading companies as members. 63 organizations are currently listed as MLCommons members, including Google, Microsoft, Nvidia, and Intel.

While MLPerf is MLCommons' most visible effort, the organization aims to advance Machine Learning in general, with benchmarking being one of the tools towards that end.

Other efforts include creating free-to-use datasets – People's Speech dataset is among the world's largest English speech recognition corpus today, and MLCube, a set of best practices for creating ML software that can easily run on different systems.

The following benchmarks are published by MLCommons under MLPerf name:

- MLPerf Training: AI training of state-of-the-art DL models used in the industry
- MLPerf Training HPC: AI training used in scientific codes executed on supercomputers
- MLPerf Inference – Data Center: AI Inference on servers
- MLPerf Inference – Edge: AI Inference on edge servers
- MLPerf Inference – Mobile: AI Inference on mobile devices such as phones and laptops
- MLPerf Inference – Tiny: AI Inference on embedded devices

Each benchmark is divided into a Closed and Open Division. The former requires that the HW-optimized models are equivalent to the reference, while no such requirement is imposed on the latter, which allows submitters to showcase their algorithmic improvements. This makes results in Closed division directly comparable as a measure of HW performance for the same problem and it usually receives more submissions than Open.

Of the benchmarks categories listed above, MLPerf Training and Inference receive, by far, most submissions. In this paper, we are focusing on these two benchmark suites, not only because of their popularity, but also because they are used for server evaluation, which is the focus area of this work.

## 3.1 MLPerf Training

MLPerf Training focuses on benchmarking AI training performance. The metric is time-to-train expressed in minutes. As of version 2.0, there are 8 benchmarks and the results for each are reported separately. This enables end users to evaluate which chip and/or server is suitable for each task. For most benchmarks, full training from scratch to achieving the predefined accuracy is measured, except for DLRM and Minigo models, where only partial training is required due to a high time cost.

Because training times vary from run to run, several runs need to be submitted. The exact numbers vary between benchmarks and are between 5 to 40. A certain number of best and worst scores are discarded and the rest are averaged to produce a published score. Submitters are allowed to choose the hyperparameters that suite their hardware, but submissions cannot converge in less epochs than the reference implementation.

## 3.2 MLPerf Inference

MLPerf Inference is measured on a single server. MLPerf provides Loadgen, a process which sends queries to the inference process, which then responds once it processes the sent data. There are several scenarios each one with its own metric as show in Table 1.

**Table 1.** MLPerf Inference scenarios.

| Inference Scenario | Metric | Inference Division |
|---|---|---|
| Offline | Throughput in Samples/second | Datacenter, Edge |
| Server | Maximum Poisson throughput parameter that satisfies latency constraint | Datacenter |
| Single Stream | $90^{th}$ percentile latency | Edge |
| MultiStream | 99th percentile latency | Edge |

# 4 TPCx-AI Benchmark

Released about a year ago, TPCx-AI represents an important step in AI workload benchmarking. TPC has a long history of creating generally accepted benchmarks that are adopted across the computing industry and are viewed as a fair evaluation of compute performance.

TPCx-AI recently proposed a single number benchmark measure to evaluate the end-to-end performance based on real world AI scenarios and data science use cases. The dataset for this benchmark comprises of the retail datacenter for an organization that contains 14 structured tables and 2 unstructured files. The benchmark covers 10 use cases relevant to retail businesses and on-premise, cloud and edge environments. The use cases all share the same dataset. The benchmark test consists of 5 test stages:

a)  Load Test: Data generation and data load, optional cleansing and transformation
b)  Power Training Test: Data preprocessing, training and model generation
c)  Power Serving Test I, Power Serving Test II: Data preprocessing, model deployment and business insight.
d)  Scoring Test: Data preprocessing, model validation. This step is not included in the benchmark metric calculation.
e)  Throughput Test: Multi-user throughput test.

When running the benchmark, all ten use cases are executed and the performance is represented by a single score, which is described in more detail below. The 10 use cases are listed the Table 2 below. A scale factor (SF), which represents a size of the generated data in GB, needs to be chosen prior to benchmark execution. Scores are reported along with SF being used for a particular submission.

**Table 2.** TPCx-AI Use Cases

| Use Case | Model | Deep AI (Y/N) |
| --- | --- | --- |
| UC1 Customer Segmentation | K-Means | N |
| UC2 Customer Conversation Transcription | Deepspeech (RNN) | Y |
| UC3 Sales Forecast | ARIMA | N |
| UC4 Spam Detection | Naïve Bayes | N |
| UC5 Price Prediction | Recurrent Neural Network (RNN) | Y |
| UC6 Hardware Failure | Support Vector Machines (SVMs) | N |
| UC7 Product Rating | Alternating Least Squares (ALS) | N |
| UC8 Classification of Trips | Classification (Model Unspecified) | ? |
| UC9 Facial Recognition | Embedding and Logistic Regression | N |
| UC10 Fraud Detection | Logistic Regression | N |

### 4.1 TPCx-AI Metric

The TPCx-AI metric is calculated using the formula below

$$AIUCpm@SF = \frac{SF * N * 60}{\sqrt[4]{T_{LD} * T_{PTT} * T_{PST} * T_{TT}}}$$

where the denominator is a geometric average of elapsed times (in seconds) representing 4 major stages of the AI workloads. Specifically:

- $T_{LD}$ is the elapsed time to copy the dataset during Load Test
- $T_{PTT}$ is the geometric average of Power Training Test elapsed times of all the use cases.
- $T_{PST}$ is the maximum of geometric averages of Power Serving Tests elapsed times for all use cases – there are 2 such tests.
- $T_{TT}$ is the average elapsed time of all the use cases executed over all concurrent streams during the throughput test. S is the predefined concurrent user sessions chosen by the test sponsor. The sequence of the use cases is randomized for each user session. $T_{T_{put}}$ is the elapsed time of all streams during the throughput test.

$$T_{TT} = \frac{1}{N * S} T_{T_{put}}$$

- SF is the scale factor proportional to the size of the dataset.
- N is the number of test cases. Currently, N = 10.

The Price/Performance Metric is simply calculated as the price divided by $AIUCpm@SF$.

## 4.2 TPCx-AI Metric Analysis

The Performance Metric aims to distill the overall performance into a single score. In the formula, the denominator represents time and thus the formula gives a measure of throughput, or rate. Therefore, a higher score indicates better system performance.

While having a single score simplifies systems comparison, it hides a lot of complexity and nuances. Below, we expand the explanation on a few elements used in the metric.

### 4.2.1 Averaging Benchmark Measure Over Multiple Use Cases

TPCx-AI benchmark used geometric mean to average the elapsed time of $N$ use cases under each test stage and to average the elapsed time of all test stages. Harmonic mean is used to calculate the final benchmark measure using the averaged elapsed time.

An accepted rule of thumb requires the average calculation to preserve the proportional relationship to the total time consumed by the benchmark expressed in units of time or preserve the inverse proportional relationship to the total time consumed by the benchmark expressed as a rate [13]. It can be shown that arithmetic mean preserves the property when measuring a set of benchmarks expressed in units of time [13]. Harmonic mean preserves the property for measuring rate [13].

An example of arithmetic mean and geometric mean for evaluating computer system performance is demonstrated in Table 3, where geometric mean incorrectly identifies SUT2 as having the best performance.

**Table 3.** Example of Comparing Arithmetic Mean and Geometric Mean. SUT 1 is the system that takes the least time to complete the tests while using Geometric mean identifies SUT2 as the winner.

| Benchmark (seconds) | SUT 1 | SUT 2 | SUT 3 |
|---|---|---|---|
| Use Case 1 | 20 | 10 | 40 |
| Use Case 2 | 45 | 80 | 45 |
| Total Time of Use Case 1&2 | 65 | 90 | 85 |
| Arithmetic Mean | 32.5 | 45 | 42.5 |
| Geometric Mean | 30 | 28.28 | 42.43 |

The example demonstrates pitfalls of using geometric mean to summarize time, which overemphasizes low values and can be a wrong tool for comparing performance. Because of this, arithmetic mean or a summation of total time might be a better choice to measure the elapsed times. Therefore, we propose the following formula as an alternative:

$$AIUCpm@SF = \frac{SF * N * 60}{T_{LD} + T_{PTT} + T_{PST} + T_{TT}}.$$

Here $T_{LD}$ remains the same as before. $T_{PTT}$ is the aggregated total elapsed time of all N use cases during Power Training Test. $T_{PST}$ is the maximum of the aggregated total elapsed time of N use cases from Power Training Test I and Test II. $T_{TT}$ is the average elapsed time per stream by tracking the total elapsed time from executing N test cases on each stream divided by the total number of concurrent streams S.

The formula measures system throughput over the end-to-end modeling process using aggregated total time in each stage. It agrees with the intuitive sense that the faster a system can handle the N test cases, the better by preserving the nice ranking properties stated above where it's inversely proportional to the total time consumed by the benchmark.

### 4.2.2   Weighting Factors for Test Stages and on Scale Factors

The metric put equal weight on all four stages being measured in the metric. However, since training is typically the most time-consuming part of AI workload, the measure is likely to be dominated by the training time. Therefore, assigning weights to the different parts of AI process may produce more realistic representation of the workload.

TPCx-AI reports scores with different values of SF separately, which means SF can be treated as a constant in the metric formula. In the future, TPCx-AI could leverage the SF to compare systems with different sizes of data using a single metric. The drawback to this approach is it assumes a linear relationship between the processing times of different sizes of data, which assumption may not always be true.

## 5   MLPerf vs TPCx-AI

The table below summarizes main differences between MLPerf and TPCx-AI that are further discussed below (Table 4).

**Table 4.**  Comparison between TPCx-AI and MLPerf

|         | Scope              | Scoring              | Results Review | CodeLicense | Cost Membership/ Submission                        | Result per Watt | Results per cost |
|---------|--------------------|----------------------|----------------|-------------|----------------------------------------------------|-----------------|------------------|
| TPCx-AI | End-to-end         | One score per SF     | Audit          | TPC-EULA    | $15,000/$500 (member) $750(non-member)             | No              | Yes              |
| MLPerf  | Training, Inference | Multiple scores     | Peer review    | Apache v2.0 | Not disclosed/$0                                   | Yes             | No               |

### 5.1   Scope and Scoring

A major difference between TPCx-AI and MLPerf benchmarks is scope. The former attempts to capture the end-to-end AI process encompassing data processing, training, and inferencing, while the latter covers only training and inference. Furthermore, MLPerf is focused on Deep Learning (DL) and state-of-the art algorithms, while TPCx-AI use cases cover both DL and non-DL cases, with majority use cases being non-DL. Additionally, MLPerf uses publicly available datasets that are many GB in size, while TPCx-AI generates data on the fly.

TCPx-AI uses a single score to characterize performance of all the end-to-end AI workloads, while MLPerf publishes multiple scores for each benchmark – for example image classification training score is separate from recommendation training score as well as from inference scores. This means that MLPerf performance evaluation is more granular, while TPCx-AI, even with its larger scope, generates a single score.

The difference in scoring and scope makes sense for each approach: state-of-the-art DL, captured by MLPerf, requires dedicated HW resources and thus considering training and inference separately is needed, while less computationally demanding AI can be deployed on multi-purpose servers, where having a single score is exactly what is needed.

## 5.2  Results Review

MLPerf results undergo a multi-week peer review process. All submitters participate and can raise issues against any other submitter. Issues that cannot be resolved between the two parties are decided by a group vote. Additionally, a submission gets randomly selected for an audit.

In contrast, TPCx-AI uses audit to verify submissions prior to publication. This means that results can be submitted and published any time, while MLPerf's peer review system requires certain time windows for submissions when all submitters get together.

## 5.3  Code License

MLPerf reference code as well as optimized code used for submissions is released under Apache license. This is a very permissive license allowing re-use and even using for commercial purposes. TPCx-AI uses a standard TPC End User License Agreement (EULA), which places significant usage restrictions. Materials associated with the benchmark can be copied, transferred or used for commercial purposes.

## 5.4  Cost

The two benchmarks have a very different cost structure. Each organization charges a membership fee, with TPC membership covering many areas of computing beyond costing $15,000 for large organization. A submission requires $500 fee for audit and publication. Submissions from non-members are allowed but cost $750. MLCommons membership cost is not disclosed, although our understanding is that it is more costly than TPC. In the other hand there is no additional fee for submission and publication. Only members can submit scores to MLPerf.

## 5.5   Efficiency Scores

Both benchmarks publish efficiency scores, but each one does it in a different way: MLPerf publishes per Watt results for inference, but this is optional and requires a special process during which a server's power is being measured. On the other hand. TPCx-AI publishes per cost results – these are applicable to all submissions and are based on list prices for computer resources used.

## 5.6   Accelerators

DL has been an accelerator-dominated field. With GPUs and other accelerators providing several times the performance of CPUs, MLPerf has become a showcase for accelerator performance. In fact, all of the submissions in the latest round of MLPerf Training are accelerated, and in the latest MLPerf Inference only 3 submissions out of 144 do not use accelerators.

In contrast, accelerators are not central to TPCx-AI. This is probably due to the end-to-end design, which includes extensive data manipulation – a task that is not suited for GPUs. In reality, demanding DL workloads would be executed in dedicated nodes with multiple accelerators, while data manipulation and non-DL ML would be executed on general purpose nodes. But such a complex setup is typically impractical as exemplified by the fact that all submissions so far are for single server with no accelerator. We expect that this will remain an issue going forward as end-to-end AI system in practice require large clusters with different types of nodes that are too costly to set up for benchmarking purposes. In that particular aspect, MLPerf's piecemeal approach may be preferable as it splits evaluation into smaller pieces.

## 5.7   When to Use Each Tool

Given the significant differences between the two benchmarks, each one is suitable for different scenario. MLPerf is tracking latest algorithmic developments in AI and evaluates only AI training and inference. Because of this, it is suitable for evaluating chips abilities to process complex neural nets. For example, a new chips manufacturer can use this benchmark to prove that their product stacks up well against incumbents in the field. A nuance here is that MLPerf scores are measured on servers and thus they reflect capabilities of servers dedicated for DL, however these can be used as a proxy for chips performance.

TPCx-AI, with the focus on the end-to-end AI process including data manipulation, is more suitable for evaluating "Big Data" systems, which handle both data manipulation, pipelines, and AI operations.

# 6   Summary and Conclusions

TPCx-AI is a recent entry into AI benchmarking tools and has to compete against established players. MLPerf is currently the most comprehensive tool that has wide acceptance among leading AI companies. This work compared both benchmarks in detail. While both tools, nominally, focus on the same area, their approaches to the problem are markedly different. Specifically, MLPerf, effectively, functions as a tool evaluating chip performance for DL training and inference, while TPCx-AI is more of a system level tool covering end-to-end AI process while covering both traditional ML as well as DL. Scoring differs between the tools, too, with MLPerf publishing a series of benchmark results for each tested platform, while TPCx-AI publishes a single number representing different parts of AI workloads and encompassing 10 different use cases. In addition, submissions, validations, and publications also differ.

For TPCx-AI we discussed the metric in detail and point out alternative ways how a score can be computed in a way that can be more reflective of the hardware.

Looking forward, we expect both tools to be used alongside each other, as their purposes are quite different. MLPerf will continue to be a testing tool for the ability of specialized chips (accelerators) to perform state-of-the-art AI, while TPCx-AI will find its place as a full system evaluation tool for all parts of the AI workloads.

# References

1. TPCx-AI. https://www.tpc.org/tpcx-ai/default5.asp.
2. Transaction Processing and Performance Council, "TPC Express Benchmark ™ AI - Full Disclosure Report" (2022)
3. Hodak, M., Ellison, D., Dholakia, A.: Benchmarking AI inference: where we are in 2020. In: 12th TPC Technology Conference (2020)
4. Hodak, M., Ellison, D., Dholakia, A.: Everyone is a winner: interpreting MLPerf inference benchmark results. In: 13th TPC Technology Conference (2021)
5. Bourrasset, C., et al.: Requirements for an enterprise AI benchmark. In: Nambiar, R., Poess, M. (eds.) TPCTC 2018. LNCS, vol. 11135, pp. 71–81. Springer, Cham (2019). https://doi.org/10.1007/978-3-030-11404-6_6
6. Bench Research, Deep Bench. https://github.com/baidu-research/DeepBench
7. Coleman, C.A., et al.: DAWNBench: an end-to-end deep learning benchmark and competition. In: Proceedings of the 31st Conference on Neural Information Processing Systems (NIPS 2017) (2017)
8. AIPerf. https://aiperf.org/
9. HPL-AI. https://hpl-ai.org/
10. MLPerf. https://mlcommons.org/
11. Mattson, P., et al.: MLPerf training benchmark. Proc. Mach. Learn. Syst. **2**, 336–349 (2020)
12. Reddy, V.J., et al.: MLPerf Inference Benchmark, arXiv preprint arXiv:1911:02549, (2019)
13. Smith, J.E.: Characterizing Computer Performance With A Single Number, Commun. ACM, **31**(10), 1202–1206 (1988). https://dl.acm.org/doi/pdf/10.1145/63039.63043

# Preliminary Scaling Characterization of TPCx-AI

Hamesh Patel, Kacper Ufa, Sammy Nah, Amandeep Raina,
and Rodrigo Escobar(✉)

Intel Corporation, Hillsboro, OR 97124, USA
{hamesh.s.patel,kacper.ufa,sammy.nah,amandeep.k.raina,
rodrigo.d.escobar.palacios}@intel.com

**Abstract.** TPCx-AI is the latest TPC benchmark addressing some of
the numerous challenges in AI benchmarking. It has the ability to scale
datasets, to emulate machine learning and deep learning end-to-end
pipelines, and to provide solutions that are commercially available with
pricing and support. With TPC benchmarks it can be difficult to get
started as the nature of system benchmarks require larger server configurations and software solutions. TPCx-AI is a TPC *Express Benchmark*
and thus provides an executable *kit* that simplifies the setup and execution of the benchmark. Moreover, the TPCx-AI kit includes two reference
implementations: one for single-node environments—using scikit-learn as
its primary ML processing library—and the other targeted for multi-node
environments—centered around the use of Spark—. This paper provides
insights into the TPCx-AI kit installation and setup steps. It also shares
preliminary scaling data of the key phases of the benchmark (e.g. pre-
processing, training, serving, etc.), distribution of the phases for each of
the use cases, and finally an example of how one can look at resource
utilization for a specific use case. We show that for the single-node implementation each of the use cases show a unique runtime distribution for
the time spent in preprocessing, training and serving phases. In addition,
we also show how the processing runtimes scale with dataset sizes as they
would in real world, with some use cases scaling poorly. We anticipate
that optimizations in the platform as well as software stack can lead to
overall reductions in runtime and expect this work to inspire others to
investigate the runtime characteristics of the ML/DL workloads included
in TPCx-AI and their possible optimizations.

**Keywords:** AI Benchmarks · Artificial Intelligence · Machine
Learning · Deep Learning · AI · TPC · Express Benchmarks ·
TPCx-AI · Runtime Performance · Scalability

## 1 Introduction

Artificial Intelligence (AI) benchmarking, and more specifically machine learning
(ML) and deep learning (DL) benchmarking[1], has gained significant relevance

---

[1] DL is a subset of ML. The term *Traditional ML* is used in this paper to categorize
the ML methods that are not part of the DL subset.

© The Author(s), under exclusive license to Springer Nature Switzerland AG 2023
R. Nambiar and M. Poess (Eds.): TPCTC 2022, LNCS 13860, pp. 78–93, 2023.
https://doi.org/10.1007/978-3-031-29576-8_6

over the last few years. The ubiquitous use of ML methods to make scientific discoveries and to extract insights from large heterogenous data in industry and academia has become substantially more mainstream and their applications a preponderant part of our daily lives [4,23]. This is in great part due to the enormous growth in the amount and variety of digital data as well as the afford-able computing capacities available to process such data [8]. With AI software and solutions being integrated into products and services, it becomes imperative that standards bodies take upon themselves to develop meaningful standards around the right use of the technology. The TPCx-AI standard addresses some key deficiencies absent in AI benchmarking to date.

Current AI benchmarks focus mainly on measuring the performance of a system or specific hardware component when training a prediction model (i.e. model training) or when making predictions with a previously trained model (i.e. serving, also called inference). However, training and serving are in general just a part of a larger AI processing pipeline. In practice, data is rarely directly used in its original form to build a AI model. Instead, data typically need to go through multiple transformations before being ready to be fed into a model building algorithm. Such set of data transformations is often called pre-processing. During pre-processing, data go through a series of steps that might include reading data into memory, copying data from one location to another, removing outliers or other unwanted data, aggregating data with some characteristics in common, merging data from different sources, or projecting data to different spaces. It's not uncommon for these transformations to take 60% or more of the whole data science pipeline execution time [18,19,23]. Nevertheless, data pre-processing is still often overlooked by current AI benchmarks. TPCx-AI addresses that gap with the implementation of representative end-to-end AI use cases that emulate the behavior of real customer scenarios with realistic datasets. The term *Use Case* in TPCx-AI refers to a particular scenario for which a model is trained and later on used for serving (i.e. for making predictions)[2]. Figure 1 shows the different parts of a sample use case training pipeline from TPCx-AI. TPCx-AI includes 10 use cases (7 ML and 3 DL), each one with a training and a serving pipeline. TPCx-AI addresses the needs of hardware innovators, software solution developers and academia where an existing AI stack could be put to test using the reference use cases [11]. Another feature of TPCx-AI is its ability to scale to large datasets which has previously been a challenge due to many

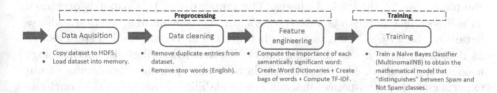

**Fig. 1.** Sample TPCx-AI training pipeline

---

[2] Serving is also commonly known as inference in the AI terminology.

**Table 1.** Differences between ML and DL algorithms

| Machine Learning | Deep Learning |
|---|---|
| Lower need for computing power | Lower need for human intervention |
| Usage of structured data | Usage of unstructured data |
| Simple algorithms | Employs neural networks |
| Engineer sets up whole classifier | Algorithm learns from its own errors |
| Can be based on smaller data sets | Larger data requirements (quality and quantity) |
| Can often be run on conventional computers | Requires more powerful hardware |
| In use in many everyday tools such as email inbox or bank | Let us get to use more complex projects like self-driving cars |
| Potentially is more likely to make mistake, because it doesn't adapt | Improves results over time with more available data |

reasons, including privacy, lack of representative data, and applicability into a benchmarking test.

Deep Learning (DL) algorithms—the subset of ML techniques based on the use of multi-layered neural networks—have captured the attention of companies, media, and researchers over the last decade [8]. These algorithms have been crucial to solving very complex tasks, such as speech-recognition, automated driving, language translation, face recognition, and natural language processing, among others [3,5]. Despite the undisputed relevance of DL algorithms, industry still relies broadly on the traditional ML algorithms[1] that have stood the test of time for decades. Compared to traditional ML algorithms, DL algorithms typically require significantly larger amounts of data and more compute power to build accurate models. In addition, DL model's output are more difficult to explain or make general statements about [6,15,23]. Table 1 presents some of the key differences between ML and DL algorithms [22]. With technological advances in hardware and software, traditional machine learning pipelines are still used broadly as for some tasks they can generate insights as accurately as a complementary deep learning model but with lower strain on hardware resources. As a result, TPCx-AI includes both ML and DL use cases relevant in today's production environments [24].

The goal of this paper is to present details about the structure of the TPCx-AI kit as well as its installation process. It also presents some of the benefits of TPCx-AI and TPC benchmarks in general and share performance results when scaling TPCx-AI from smaller datasets to larger ones, and the time it takes to complete some of the critical phases. The remainder of this paper is organized as follows: Sect. 2 presents related work on AI benchmarks. Section 3 shares details on the TPCx-AI kit, including installation and configuration steps as well as details on how to run the benchmark. Section 4 describes the methodology used to test and collect performance data. It also presents the results of our experiments in performance analysis and scalability. Finally, Sect. 5 concludes the paper and presents possible future work.

## 2   Related Work

The impact of AI applications in industry and daily life has triggered the creation of several benchmarks for AI. In this section we present relevant work in the area of systems benchmarking for AI workloads. That is, benchmarks that characterize the maximum performance a SUT can reach when running AI workloads. Other types of AI benchmarks are essentially datasets which purpose is to evaluate the quality of ML models [7,14,25], or to evaluate the performance of a specific hardware or software component [13,21].

MLPerf is a benchmark composed of two different benchmark suites: MLPerf Training [16] and MLPerf inference [20]. Both suites include metrics and methods to measure and compare the performance of hardware and software components for tasks such as computer vision, natural language processing, recommendation, and reinforcement learning. Deepbench [1] is a benchmarking tool that can be used to measure the performance of hardware on basic operations, such as matrix multiplications, convolutions, recurrent layers, and communication primitives that are fundamental to DL workloads. HiBench [2] is a big data benchmark suite developed by Intel® that includes 27 workloads (as of version 7.1.1), including 6 micro benchmarks, 1 SQL, 2 websearch, 1 graph, 4 streaming, and 13 ML workloads. Bayesian classification, K-Means, logistic regression, Alternating Least Squares (ALS), and Support Vector Machines (SVM) are part of the ML workloads included in HIBench. AIBench [9] is a benchmark suite with 19 tasks from different AI domains: image classification, image generation, text-to-text translation, image-to-text, image-to-image, among others. AIBench presumes the performance of real-world end-to-end application scenarios can be abstracted based on the execution of one or more of such tasks. TBD [26]— short for Training Benchmark for DNNs—is a benchmark suite that focuses on DNN training on GPUs for six ML applications: image classification, machine translation, speech recognition, object detection, adversarial networks, and reinforcement learning. BigDataBench [10] is a big data and AI benchmark that, as of version 5.0, provides 13 representative real-world data sets and 27 big data benchmarks. ML related workloads include bayes classification, KMeans and Latent Dirichlet Allocation (LDA).

TPCx-AI is a benchmark that includes a runnable implementation provided by the TPC. The benchmark includes 10 end-to-end use cases covering both traditional ML and DL algorithms. Furthermore, by being a TPC benchmark, results need to be verified by a TPC-certified benchmark auditor before being published and require providing total system pricing.

## 3   TPCx-AI Kit

TPCx-AI is a TPC (Transaction Processing Council) *Express Benchmark* addressing some of the numerous challenges in AI benchmarking. As of v1.0.2 it comprises 10 end-to-end use cases (7 ML and 3 DL) that are relevant in current production datacenters and cloud environments. Table 2 presents details of the 10 end-to-end use cases included in TPCx-AI.

**Table 2.** TPCx-AI use cases (version 1.0.2)

| ID | Use-case | Description | ML/DL |
|---|---|---|---|
| UC01 | Customer Segmentation | Clustering/segmentation of customers based on return behavior (return frequency, return/order ratio, ...); Clustering/segmentation of customers based on buying behavior (frequency of purchases, recency of purchases, ...) | ML |
| UC02 | Speech To Text | Processing audio recordings from support hotline to label and prioritize services/products | DL |
| UC03 | Sales Prediction | Predict sales for departments within Walmart based on historical sales and markdown event | ML |
| UC04 | Spam Detection | Detect comments/reviews/descriptions with spam content | ML |
| UC05 | Price Prediction | Predict product price based on textual description | DL |
| UC06 | Detect hardware failure in data center | Based on past knowledge about hardware utilization, predict hardware failure | ML |
| UC07 | Product Recommendation | Improve cross-selling by giving "next-to-buy" recommendations | ML |
| UC08 | Trip Type Classification | Predict the trip type (weekly grocery shopping, dinner party shopping) based on purchases (items, item categories) and the weekday | ML |
| UC09 | Face recognition | Find the identity of people from face images | DL |
| UC10 | Detect Fraudulent Transactions | Detect fraudulent transaction based on historic data of transactions | ML |

TPCx-AI includes an executable *kit* that is available for download from the TPC website. The term *kit* refers to the predefined executable implementation released with every TPC *Express Benchmark* (e.g. TPCx-BB, TPCx-IoT, etc.) [12]. *Express Benchmarks* were introduced by the TPC in 2013 in an effort to make their benchmarks easier to comply with and to run compared to the other—more traditional—category of TPC benchmarks known as TPC *Enterprise Benchmarks*. Unlike *Express Benchmarks*, TPC *Enterprise Benchmarks* typically require the development of a benchmark implementation not provided by the TPC [17]. In the case of TPCx-AI, its kit is composed of routines and software utilities that generate synthetic data, verify the integrity of the files included in the kit, execute the aforementioned 10 ML/DL use cases for the required benchmark tests, compute the results, provide some level of validation about the execution of the benchmark, and collect information about the runtime environment (e.g. Operating system distribution, network interface configuration, number of nodes used, software versions, etc.), among other functionalities. Furthermore, the TPCx-AI kit includes two implementations of the benchmark. The first implementation targets execution on a single node and is centered around the use of widely-used AI Python libraries (e.g. Scikit-Learn, Pandas, Keras and Tensorflow). The second implementation is targeted for multi-node environments and is centered around the use of Spark, MLLib, Tensorflow and Horovod. Users can choose to execute either of the two implementations depending on their needs and interests. The TPCx-AI benchmark specification defines some rules about comparability of different benchmark runs[3] [24].

---

[3] For instance, cross-implementation results are not allowed to be compared as per the rules of the benchmark.

**Table 3.** Description of the top-level kit files and directories

| File/Directory | Description |
| --- | --- |
| bin | Location of the tpcxai.sh script used by the TPCx-AI_Benchmarkrun.sh script to run the benchmark. |
| data-gen | Location of the data generator (PDGF) |
| driver | Contains the benchmark driver (i.e. The code that controls the execution of the benchmark from beginning to end. |
| lib | Library files included with the benchmark. |
| output | This directory contains the output of the data generator. It is created the first time the benchmark is run. It is also where the output of the use cases is stored when running the single-node implementation. |
| setenv.sh | Configuration file for configuration parameters that impact the overall execution of the benchmark. |
| setup-python.sh | Installs the libraries and software packages necessary to run the single-node implementation of the benchmark. |
| setup-spark.sh | Installs the libraries and software packages necessary to run the multi-node implementation of the benchmark. |
| tools | Location of several utilities needed to run the benchmark and generate the results report. |
| TPCx-AI_Benchmarkrun.sh | Script that starts the execution of the benchmark. |
| TPCx-AI_Validation.sh | Script that starts the execution of the benchmark using Scale Factor 1. |
| workload | Contains the source code of the benchmark use cases |

## 3.1   Licensing and Setup

In order to run TPCx-AI users must sign-up and agree to the TPCx-AI End User Licensing Agreement (EULA) before downloading the kit from the tpc.org website [24]. All related work (such as collaterals, papers, derivatives) must acknowledge the TPC and include the TPCx-AI copyright. The TPCx-AI kit is distributed in compressed format (e.g. zip file, tarball, etc.). Once downloaded, the kit content can be extracted to a local directory. The directory contains the TPCx-AI specification document, the TPCx-AI Users Guide (README.md) documentation, scripts to set up the benchmark environment, code to execute the benchmark workload, a synthetic data generator, use case related files, and the benchmark driver. A description of the most relevant files and subdirectories of the TPCx-AI kit is presented in Table 3. For the single-node implementation users need to run the *setup-python.sh* script. Similarly, users interested in running the multi-node implementation need to run the *setup-spark.sh* script. These scripts will initiate the setup process to install the libraries and software packages necessary to run the benchmark.

## 3.2   Configuration

Once the benchmark setup is finished, users need to provide several configuration parameters that would determine the way the benchmark will be run and whose specific values depend on the interests of the users and their System Under Test (SUT). The *setenv.sh* file can be used to set higher level configuration parameters that would impact the overall execution of the benchmark. In addition, a YAML file needs to be provided containing configuration parameters that may impact the execution of individual use cases as well as other global parameters, including variables that specify filesystem and use case code location, paths to the input datasets, and the output locations for the training, serving and scoring phases. The location of the YAML file itself must be provided as a parameter in the *setenv.sh* file as described below. Sample default YAML configuration files for both the single-node and the multi-node implementations are provided in the kit under the *driver/configs* directory and are helpful as a reference for users to ensure all user parameters are set correctly.

The following benchmark parameters can be set in the *setenv.sh* script:

- *TPCxAI_SCALE_FACTOR*: This parameter determines the scale factor (i.e. the approximate size in gigabytes) of the synthetic data set that will be generated and that will be the input to the use cases execution. Users can select any scale factor of the form $1 \times 10^x$ or $3 \times 10^x$ where $x$ is a non-negative integer[4].
- *TPCxAI_SERVING_THROUGHPUT_STREAMS*: This parameter determines the number of parallel streams for the SERVING_THROUGHPUT test (See Sect. 3.3 for a description of the set of tests required to be run for a result to be considered valid).
- *TPCxAI_CONFIG_FILE_PATH*: This parameter is used by the test sponsor to specify the configuration file that will be used to run the benchmark.
- *TPCxAI_ENV_TOOLS_DIR*: Location of the directory containing scripts to collect system configuration information. By convention this is a subdirectory of the tools directory.
- *YARN_CONF_DIR*: Location of the YARN configuration directory for multi-node environments[5].
- *PYSPARK_PYTHON*: Python executable used by the *Spark* workers for the execution of DL use cases. This must be accessible to all *Spark* workers[5].
- *PYSPARK_DRIVER_PYTHON*: Python executable used by the *Spark* driver for the execution of DL use cases. This must be accessible to the driver node[5].

## 3.3   Benchmark Execution

After making all the required configurations as described in Sects. 3.1 and 3.2, the *TPCx-AI_Benchmarkrun.sh* bash script at the root of the benchmark directory must be used to execute the benchmark in its entirety. Figure 2 presents the workflow of the benchmark execution. The following 6 tests are required to be run by the TPCx-AI benchmark in order to obtain a valid result:

---

[4] Our experiments have shown the data generator being able to generate datasets ranging from 1 GB to 10 TB. However, it's theoretically possible for the data generator to generate up to hundreds of PB.

[5] Applies only to the multi-node implementation.

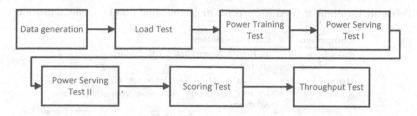

**Fig. 2.** TPCx-AI tests workflow

- *Load Test*: This test measures the time it takes the SUT to copy the input dataset files to the final location from where they will eventually be accessed to execute the subsequent benchmark tests.
- *Power Training Test*: This test determines the maximum speed the SUT can process the training phase of all 10 use cases by measuring the time it takes to run them in sequence.
- *Power Serving Test I and Power Serving Test II*: Power Serving tests determine the maximum speed the SUT can process the serving phase of all 10 use cases by measuring the time it takes to run them in sequence. After running both Power Serving tests only the one with the longest runtime is used to compute the final metric. The result of the other test is discarded.
- *Scoring Test*: This test is used to measure the quality of the predictions made by the models created in the Power Training Test. Each use case must meet a predefined quality metric threshold. The predefined quality metrics and their threshold values can be found in the benchmark specification [24].
- *Throughput Test*: This test measures the ability of the SUT to run a high number of concurrent serving pipelines in the least amount of time.

Before any of the tests are run, the *TPCx-AI_Benchmarkrun.sh* will run a phase called *Data Generation* to generate the input dataset that will be used in all the benchmark tests. The amount of data in gigabytes that is generated is specified by the *TPCxAI_SCALE_FACTOR* parameter that was introduced in Sect. 3.2. The input dataset for the benchmark is generated by the PDGF (Parallel Data Generator Framework) utility that is included in the benchmark kit. PDGF generates different input datasets for the Power Training, the Power Serving and the Scoring tests. The Throughput Test uses the same input datasets as the Power Serving tests. All PDGF generated data is written to the *output* subdirectory.

## 4 Performance Results

In this section we present the results of our experiments for single-node and multi-node setups in terms of scaling and resource utilization.

### 4.1 System Under Test (SUT)

Table 4 presents the details of the systems used for the execution of the single-node implementation. Similarly, Table 5 lists the characteristics of the equipment used for the execution of the multi-node implementation

**Table 4.** Equipment used for execution of the single node implementation

| Component | Characteristics |
|---|---|
| Processors | 2x Intel® Xeon 8380 CPU 2.3 GHz |
| Cores/Threads | 80/160 |
| Memory — Disk | 512 GB RAM — 2x NVMe 800 GB |
| Network | 1 × 10 Gbps Intel® Ethernet Network Adapter |
| Software | Ubuntu 18.04 (kernel 5.4), python 3.8.5, Tensorflow 2.4.1 |

**Table 5.** Equipment used for execution of the multi-node implementation

| Component | Characteristics |
|---|---|
| Processors | 2x Intel® Xeon® Gold 6348 CPU @ 2.60 GHz |
| Cores/Threads | 56/112 per node (3 nodes) |
| Memory — Disk | 512 GB RAM — 6x NVMe 3.5 TB + 2x NVMe 800 GB |
| Network | 1 × 10 Gbps Intel® Ethernet Network Adapter |
| Software | Ubuntu 20.04 (kernel 5.4.0), Spark 2.4 and Spark 3.2 |

## 4.2   Single-node Implementation

With the single-node implementation, we ran multiple tests with different scale factors. All the measurements were run on a single 2-socket server. With the first set of experiments, we ran with a scale factor of 10. For the purposes of our performance characterization we just ran the Power Training Test and the Power Serving Test I of the benchmark so that we can understand each use case in more depth and break up the phases with respect to the execution time. The phases are pre-processing, training and serving.

As we can see in Fig. 3, when running with a scale factor of 10, we see that for 5 of the use cases, there is a significant amount of time spent in pre-processing the dataset before the data is used for training and serving phases. Use case 1, Use case 3, Use case 8, Use case 9 and Use case 10 show greater than 70% of the time spent on pre-processing. Use case 4, Use case 5, Use case 6 and Use case 7 spend the most time on training. Use case 6 time distribution shows that a good percentage of the execution time is spent in serving.

The distribution mimics real world challenges where a major portion of the time data scientists spend is to prepare and cleanse the data before it is ready for training and serving. TPCx-AI includes this phase in the end-to-end training and serving pipelines as well as a parameter in the overall metric calculation. The overall distribution of phases across the 10 use cases shows their runtime profile diversity and that no single use case would be a sufficient proxy for all of the AI scenarios.

As we scale from sf =1 to sf = 10, and we divide our analysis into three parts. Firstly for the pre-processing time, we see that mostly all use cases scale really well as we scale from sf = 1 to sf = 3. Use case 2 does not scale in processing time thereby showing that even though the dataset may be scaling, the compute resources may be sufficiently enough to process the data quickly. As we scale to

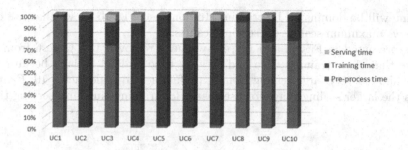

**Fig. 3.** Distribution of the time spent for each phase (preprocessing, training and serving)

scale factor 10, we see reasonable scaling of the pre-processing time for each use case. Use case 7 shows an anomaly where the time spent in preprocessing for sf = 10 is less than the time spent on preprocessing for sf = 3. We suspect that this may be as a result of the run to run variance between subsequent runs. We also expect that the processing time will increase as we increase to very large scale factors. With this being the early stages of the benchmark, more software optimizations and efficient use of the hardware should reduce the processing times drastically.

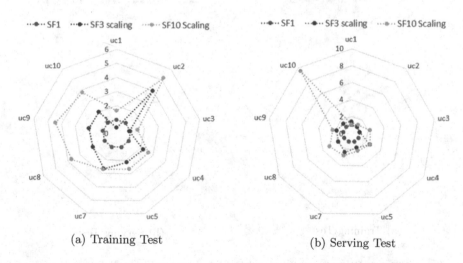

(a) Training Test                 (b) Serving Test

**Fig. 4.** Runtime scaling (single node) with varying scale factor (Use Case 6 not included)

Secondly, training times also scale effectively as we increase from scale factor 1 to scale factor 3, and to scale factor 10. In Fig. 4a, we notice that for use case 2, the training time scales highest suggesting that a majority of the time in the pipeline will be dominated by training. In contrast, Fig. 4b shows that use case 10 shows maximum scaling for serving results.

As presented in Fig. 4a and Fig. 4b, we have removed Use Case 6 from the graphs that show training time and serving time scaling. This is because use case 6 showed very large scaling from scale factor 1 to scale factor 10. Figure 5 shows the larger scaling range for use case 6 for training time and serving time.

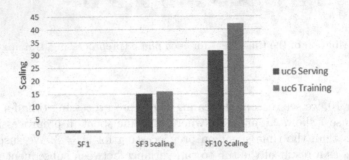

**Fig. 5.** Use Case 6 – Training and serving time scaling with scale factors (single-node)

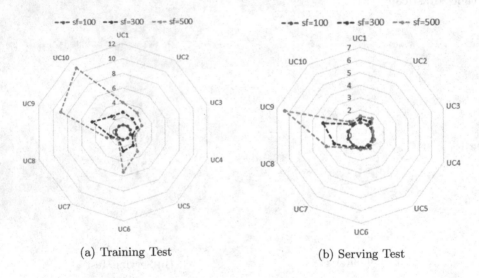

(a) Training Test                                (b) Serving Test

**Fig. 6.** Runtime scaling (multinode) with varying scale factor

### 4.3   Multinode Implementation

With the multi-node configuration we were able to run with three scale factors: 100, 300 and 500. Although scale factor 500 is not a supported TPCx-AI configuration (see Sect. 3.2), due to the lack of RAID storage configuration, we would

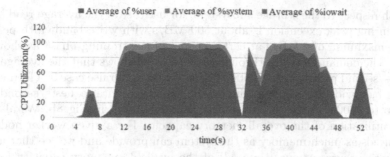

**Fig. 7.** CPU utilization over time during training for Use Case 3 (multinode)

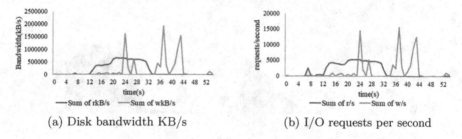

(a) Disk bandwidth KB/s    (b) I/O requests per second

**Fig. 8.** Average I/O statistics during training for Use Case 3 (multinode)

only be able to generate a dataset size for scale factor 500 or lower. Due to the lazy execution properties of Spark, we are not able to measure the pre-processing time separately during training or serving phases of the benchmark. As a result preprocessing time is included in the training and serving time.

Figure 6a shows the scaling results for training times for each of the 10 use cases when run in a Spark environment. We notice that UC9 scales proportionately to the increase in dataset size. This is followed by use case 8.

Similarly for serving test results as seen in Fig. 6b, Use case 9 and use case 10 serving times are higher than the ratio of the scale factors (from 100 to 300 to 500). From these results, we expect that the training and serving times will proportionally grow as scale factors increase.

We are able to review resource utilization for some of the use cases while running the training and serving phases. In this paper we highlight Use Case 3 for our study. Use case 3 is designed to emulate weekly sales forecasting for up to 1 year for each department [24]. It uses the multiple regression model ARIMA (Auto-Regressive Integrated Moving Average) to forecast weekly sales.

Use case 3 performance data for training in Fig. 7 shows that a majority of the training time incurs high CPU costs. On average we see that close to 50% of the time the CPU utilization is very close to 100% and the amount of time spent in *iowait* is minimal. We also see very symmetrical utilization behavior for all the nodes used for the benchmark run.

With respect to the storage subsystem, for use case 3, the average read bandwidth during peak execution is about 500 MB/s with write bandwidth peaking up to a maximum of 2 GB/s at certain times of the training phase as shown in Fig. 8a. The demand for disk throughput on Fig. 8a shows that the average read requests/second peaks at about 6000 requests/second for use case 3. The increase in write bandwidth in Fig. 8a is due to the increased write requests/second that peak up to 16000 writes/second during training shown in Fig. 8b. We also see a good utilization of the overall memory capacity. For a given worker node use case 3 needs as much memory as the system can provide and we see that as the benchmark progresses over time, all of the available memory capacity for the node is consumed.

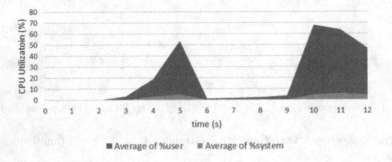

**Fig. 9.** CPU utilization over time during serving for Use Case 3 (multinode)

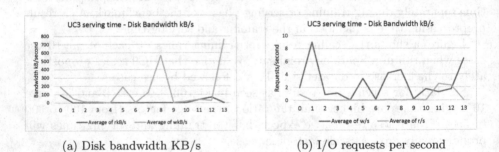

(a) Disk bandwidth KB/s          (b) I/O requests per second

**Fig. 10.** Average I/O statistics during serving for Use Case 3 (multinode)

With the serving tests, as the datasets are smaller compared to the training datasets, we see reduced serving time overall for all the use cases.

In the case of use case 3, we see an average utilization close to 30% with a peak utilization value at about 69% during the serving phase as show in Fig. 9. We expect that additional optimizations on the stack and further tuning will lead to reduced serving times and increase usage of the compute resources.

With the serving test in use case 3, we see minimal disk bandwidth in Fig. 10a suggesting that most of the execution requires minimal disk I/O (reads or writes).

With most of the I/O rate being very low as seen in Fig. 10b, we can infer that for use case 3 serving (inference) the working set fits in the physical memory available in the node.

## 5    Conclusions and Future Work

Since the launch of TPCx-AI there have been recent result publications that give us a glimpse into the performance of an end-to-end system benchmark with a set configuration. In this paper we introduced details on setting up and configuring TPCx-AI so readers can familiarize themselves with the TPCx-AI kit and can independently run experiments and conduct research. We show preliminary distribution of the time spent in preprocessing, training and serving for each of the use cases when running with the single-node implementation. We summarized the runtime results as we scale to larger scale factors for both the single-node implementation and the multi-node implementation showing that runtime for preprocessing, training and serving increase for most of the use cases as the dataset size increases. We highlight the hardware resource consumption for one of the Spark nodes as it executes Pipeline 3. Our results show that TPCx-AI scales well with increasing scale factors.

The set of results that we present in this paper are based mostly on the default settings of the sample configuration YAML files that are included in the TPCx-AI kit. By changing the configuration values a different runtime profile may be obtained. Finding the optimal configuration values for our setup was out of the scope of this paper. Additionally, as the dependency libraries used by TPCx-AI evolve, we'd expect better runtimes to be obtained. For instance, we noticed some of the libraries required by the single-node implementation started to show inefficiencies when running with larger scale factors (sf > 10). One of the goals of TPCx-AI is also to drive the evolution of its dependency libraries to better utilize the underlying hardware resources.

In future studies we will conduct a deeper analysis on each of the use cases and how optimizations both on the hardware platform as well as the software stack could elevate the performance of the benchmark and improve efficiency as well as scaling with larger datasets.

## References

1. Baidu DeepBench. https://svail.github.io/DeepBench/
2. HiBench Suite. https://github.com/Intel-bigdata/HiBench
3. Abdullah, T., Ahmet, A.: Deep learning in sentiment analysis: a survey of recent architectures. ACM Comput. Surv. 55, 3548772 (2022). https://doi.org/10.1145/3548772
4. Araujo, T., Helberger, N., Kruikemeier, S., de Vreese, C.H.: In AI we trust? Perceptions about automated decision-making by artificial intelligence. AI Soc. 35(3), 611–623 (2020). https://doi.org/10.1007/s00146-019-00931-w

5. Balafas, V., Ploskas, N.: Computational comparison of deep learning algorithms for object detection. In: 25th Pan-Hellenic Conference on Informatics, pp. 79–83. ACM, Volos Greece (Nov 2021). https://doi.org/10.1145/3503823.3503838
6. Cai, C.J., Jongejan, J., Holbrook, J.: the effects of example-based explanations in a machine learning interface. In: Proceedings of the 24th International Conference on Intelligent User Interfaces. pp. 258–262. IUI 2019, Association for Computing Machinery, New York, NY, USA (2019). https://doi.org/10.1145/3301275.3302289. event-place: Marina del Ray, California
7. Deng, J., Dong, W., Socher, R., Li, L.J., Li, K., Fei-Fei, L.: ImageNet: a large-scale hierarchical image database. In: 2009 IEEE Conference on Computer Vision and Pattern Recognition, pp. 248–255 (2009). https://doi.org/10.1109/CVPR.2009.5206848
8. Deuschle, V., Alexandrov, A., Januschowski, T., Markl, V.: End-to-end benchmarking of deep learning platforms. In: Nambiar, R., Poess, M. (eds.) TPCTC 2019. LNCS, vol. 12257, pp. 116–132. Springer, Cham (2020). https://doi.org/10.1007/978-3-030-55024-0_8
9. Gao, W., et al.: AIBench: towards scalable and comprehensive datacenter AI benchmarking. In: Zheng, C., Zhan, J. (eds.) Bench 2018. LNCS, vol. 11459, pp. 3–9. Springer, Cham (2019). https://doi.org/10.1007/978-3-030-32813-9_1
10. Gao, W., et al.: BigDataBench: a scalable and unified big data and AI benchmark suite. arXiv: Distributed. Parallel, and Cluster Computing (2018)
11. Goodfellow, I., McDaniel, P., Papernot, N.: Making machine learning robust against adversarial inputs. Commun. ACM 61(7), 56–66 (2018)
12. Huppler, K., Johnson, D.: TPC express – a new path for TPC benchmarks. In: Nambiar, R., Poess, M. (eds.) TPCTC 2013. LNCS, vol. 8391, pp. 48–60. Springer, Cham (2014). https://doi.org/10.1007/978-3-319-04936-6_4
13. Liu, L., Wu, Y., Wei, W., Cao, W., Sahin, S., Zhang, Q.: Benchmarking deep learning frameworks: design considerations, metrics and beyond, pp. 1258–1269 (2018). https://doi.org/10.1109/ICDCS.2018.00125
14. Malakar, P., Balaprakash, P., Vishwanath, V., Morozov, V., Kumaran, K.: Benchmarking machine learning methods for performance modeling of scientific applications. In: 2018 IEEE/ACM Performance Modeling, Benchmarking and Simulation of High Performance Computer Systems (PMBS), pp. 33–44 (2018). https://doi.org/10.1109/PMBS.2018.8641686
15. Manyika, J., Bughin, J.: The promise and challenge of the age of artificial intelligence. McKinsey & Company (2018). https://www.mckinsey.com/featured-insights/artificial-intelligence/the-promise-and-challenge-of-the-age-of-artificial-intelligence
16. Mattson, P., et al.: MLPerf Training Benchmark (2019). _eprint: 1910.01500
17. Nambiar, R., et al.: TPC state of the council 2013. In: Nambiar, R., Poess, M. (eds.) TPCTC 2013. LNCS, vol. 8391, pp. 1–15. Springer, Cham (2014). https://doi.org/10.1007/978-3-319-04936-6_1
18. Posoldova, A.: Machine learning pipelines: from research to production. IEEE Potentials 39(6), 38–42 (2020). https://doi.org/10.1109/MPOT.2020.3016280
19. Rabl, T., et al.: ADABench - towards an industry standard benchmark for advanced analytics. In: Nambiar, R., Poess, M. (eds.) TPCTC 2019. LNCS, vol. 12257, pp. 47–63. Springer, Cham (2020). https://doi.org/10.1007/978-3-030-55024-0_4
20. Reddi, V.J., et al.: MLPerf Inference Benchmark (2019). _eprint: 1911.02549
21. Reuther, A., Michaleas, P., Jones, M., Gadepally, V., Samsi, S., Kepner, J.: Survey and benchmarking of machine learning accelerators. In: 2019 IEEE High Perfor-

mance Extreme Computing Conference (HPEC). IEEE (2019). https://doi.org/10.1109/hpec.2019.8916327

22. Sarker, I.H.: Deep learning: a comprehensive overview on techniques, taxonomy, applications and research directions. SN Comput. Sci. **2**(6), 420 (2021). https://doi.org/10.1007/s42979-021-00815-1, https://link.springer.com/10.1007/s42979-021-00815-1

23. Storey, V.C., Lukyanenko, R., Maass, W., Parsons, J.: Explainable AI. Commun. ACM **65**(4), 27–29 (2022). place: New York, NY, USA Publisher: Association for Computing Machinery https://doi.org/10.1145/3490699

24. Transaction Processing Performance Council.: TPC Express AI - TPCx-AI Standard Specification Version 1.0.2 (2022). https://www.tpc.org/tpc_documents_current_versions/pdf/tpcx-ai_v1.0.2.pdf

25. Wang, A., Singh, A., Michael, J., Hill, F., Levy, O., Bowman, S.R.: GLUE: a multi-task benchmark and analysis platform for natural language Understanding (2019)

26. Zhu, H., et al.: TBD: benchmarking and analyzing deep neural network training. ArXiv abs/1803.06905 (2018)

# 4mbench: Performance Benchmark of Manufacturing Business Database

Kazuo Goda[1]([✉])(iD), Yuto Hayamizu[1](iD), Norifumi Nishikawa[2],
and Shinji Fujiwara[2]

[1] The University of Tokyo, Meguro-ku, Tokyo, Japan
kgoda@tkl.iis.u-tokyo.ac.jp
[2] Hitachi, Ltd., Yokohama, Kanagawwa, Japan

**Abstract.** A massive number of networked sensors are incorporated into the manufacturing business field, enabling its whole manufacturing process to be monitored and transformed into digital records. Intensive analysis of these digital assets has the potential to offer novel solutions: identifying a problematic piece of the production line and reducing its yield loss. This paper presents *4mbench*, a performance benchmark for decision support database in the manufacturing business. 4mbench has employed the 4m (man, machine, material and method) model in order to organize manufacturing event records into relational database and allow business questions to be queried on those event records. This paper presents an overall design of 4mbench that simulates food processing and packaging business operations; specifically, a database schema, a dataset generation rule and a set of queries are introduced. In addition, this paper presents an experimental case study that we conducted with 4mbench on PostgreSQL. This study revealed that the existing query optimization might yield detrimental query execution plans that offered significantly (up to four orders of magnitude) longer execution time. We hope that 4mbench provides researchers and developers with opportunities to explore the scope of further performance optimization on manufacturing business database.

**Keywords:** Database benchmark · performance measurement · manufacturing industry · 4m model

## 1 Introduction

A massive number of networked sensors are incorporated into the manufacturing business field, enabling its whole manufacturing process to be monitored and transformed into digital records [15,17,21]. Intensive analysis of these digital assets has the potential to offer novel solutions: identifying a problematic piece of the production line and reducing its yield loss [9,23]. The understanding of the data generated in the manufacturing business and the business questions posed on the data is likely helpful for the study on data management technology.

© The Author(s), under exclusive license to Springer Nature Switzerland AG 2023
R. Nambiar and M. Poess (Eds.): TPCTC 2022, LNCS 13860, pp. 94–109, 2023.
https://doi.org/10.1007/978-3-031-29576-8_7

This paper presents *4mbench*, a performance benchmark that simulates a manufacturing business database. Based on our experience, 4mbench has employed the *4m* (man, machine, material and method) model [3] in order to organize manufacturing event records into relational database and allow business questions to be queried on those event records. This paper presents a design framework of 4mbench such as a database schema, a dataset generation rule and test queries that simulate business operations of food processing and packaging. We further present the experiments that we conducted by applying 4mbench into PostgreSQL. 4mbench is disclosed at the public repository [4]; readers can reproduce and extend similar experiments on their own environments.

The rest of this paper is organized as follows. Section 2 describes the 4m model for manufacturing business. Section 3 presents the overall design of 4mbench. Section 4 presents an experimental study in which we ran 4mbench on PostgreSQL. Section 5 describes the related work, and finally Sect. 6 concludes the paper.

## 2    Description of the Manufacturing Business Based on the 4m Model

The 4m (man, machine, material and method) model is a modeling framework to describe and analyze a manufacturing business process [3]. This approach was originally a troubleshooting and risk-management method that was widely utilized in manufacturing [2,22]. Recently, the 4m model has been applied to the data management in the same business field, because it is useful to clearly describe entities that are engaged in the manufacturing business process and their relationships. This section briefly introduces the description of the manufacturing business process that we have defined based on the 4m model.

**Definition 1 (manufacturing business process).** *A manufacturing business process is composed of one or more manufacturing operations.*

**Definition 2 (manufacturing operation).** *Each manufacturing operation is operated by a worker (man), a piece of equipment (machine), and a procedure (method). It iteratively conducts an operation unit: receiving one or more incoming materials from one or more other manufacturing operations or a depository, producing one or more outgoing materials, and then delivering them to one or more other manufacturing operations or a depository.*

**Definition 3 (manufacturing event record).** *Every time completing an operation unit, each manufacturing operation produces an event record, which describes the operation unit and the incoming and outgoing materials.*

Figure 1 presents a example diagram describing a manufacturing business process based on the 4m model. This business process is composed of four manufacturing operations (Op#1, Op#2a, Op#2b and Op#3), each of which works as follows.

96     K. Goda et al.

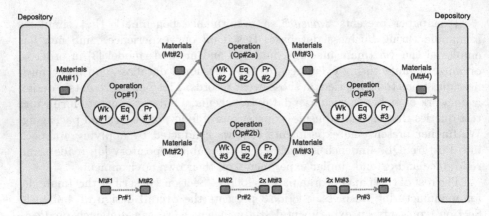

**Fig. 1.** An example diagram describing a manufacturing business process based on the 4m model. The business process is composed of four manufacturing operations (Op#1, Op#2a, Op#2b and Op#3), which are operated by three workers (Wk#1, Wk#2 and Wk#3) with three pieces of equipment (Eq#1, Eq#2 and Eq#3) and three procedures (Pr#1, Pr#2 and Pr#3). The business process consumes raw materials (Mt#1) and produces final products (Mt#4).

- Op#1 is operated by a worker (Wk#1) and an equipment (Eq#1) according to a procedure (Pr#1). Op#1 iteratively receives a material (Mt#1) from the depository, produces another material (Mt#2) and delivers it to Op#2a or Op#2b.
- Op#2a and Op#2b are both operated by an equipment (Eq#2) according to a procedure (Pr#2), but Op#2a and Op#2b are operated by different workers (Wk#2 and Wk#3) respectively. Op#2a and Op#2b iteratively receive a material (Mt#2) from Op#1, produces two materials (Mt#3) and deliver them to Op#3.
- Op#3 is operated by a worker (Wk#1) (also working for Op#1) and an equipment (Eq#3) according to a procedure (Pr#3). Op#3 iteratively receives two materials (Mt#3) from Op#2a or Op#2b, produces another material (Mt#4) and delivers it to the depository.

This example is made simple for readers' convenience. In reality, the diagram could be more complicated; for example, different workers and pieces of equipment may be engaged in the same procedure. Even in such cases, the 4m model allows us to clearly describe entities that are engaged in the business process and their relationships.

## 3   4mbench

4mbench is a performance benchmark that we have developed to simulate a manufacturing business database. The benchmark specifies a database schema, a dataset generation rule and a set of queries. This section presents an overall design of the benchmark. The detailed specification and the implementation are disclosed at a public repository [4].

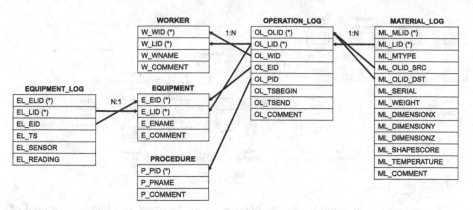

**Fig. 2.** Database schema of 4mbench. The schema is composed of three dimension tables (WORKER, EQUIPMENT and PROCEDURE) and three fact tables (OPERATION_LOG, MATERIAL_LOG and EQUIPMENT_LOG). An asterisk symbol (*) denotes that an attribute belongs to the primary key set. An arrow denotes a reference between tables.

## 3.1 Database Schema

We have designed a database schema in order to allow relational database to organize event records generated in the manufacturing business process and to answer business questions on those event records.

Figure 2 presents the database schema that we have designed on the basis of the 4m model. The schema is composed of three dimension tables and three fact tables. The three dimension tables (WORKER, EQUIPMENT and PROCEDURE) respectively describe contextual information on workers (i.e., men), equipments (i.e., machines) and procedures (i.e., methods) involved in the manufacturing business process. A fact table (OPERATION_LOG) stores an event record describing each operation unit; each record contains the association with its related worker, equipment and procedure, and time information of a concerned operation unit. Another fact table (MATERIAL_LOG) stores an event record describing each of the incoming and outgoing materials to/from the operation unit; each record contains the association with its related operation units (i.e., producer and consumer) and sensor readings (e.g., dimensions and weight) of a concerned material. EQUIPMENT_LOG is an additional fact table, which stores event records describing a status (e.g., equipment temperature) that is periodically monitored for each equipment[1].

## 3.2 Business Case and Dataset Generation

4mbench offers a dataset generator, which synthetically generates a scaled dataset to be directly imported to the database schema.

---

[1] Potentially, the schema may be further composed of similar fact tables that store status information of workers and procedures. We have omitted them for benchmark simplicity.

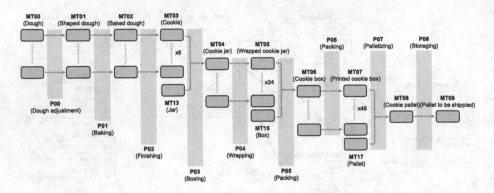

**Fig. 3.** Food processing and packaging business. This business pipeline is composed of nine procedures (P00 to P08), which produce final products (MT09) from raw materials (MT00).

**Table 1.** Nine procedures defined in 4mbench.

| Procedure # | Description (a task in each operation unit) |
|---|---|
| P00 | Dough adjustment: takes a piece of dough (MT00) from the depository and shapes the piece. |
| P01 | Baking: bakes a shaped piece of dough (MT01). |
| P02 | Finishing: performs finishing on a baked piece of dough (MT02). |
| P03 | Boxing: takes a jar (MT13) from the depository and packs six cookies (MT03) into the jar. |
| P04 | Wrapping: wraps the cookie jar (MT04). |
| P05 | Packing: takes a box (MT15) from the depository and packs 24 cookie jars (MT05) into the box. |
| P06 | Printing: makes prints on the cookie box (MT06). |
| P07 | Palletizing: takes a pallet (MT17) from the depository and stores 48 cookie boxes (MT07) into the pallet. |
| P08 | Storaging: moves a pallet (MT08) to the depository |

The 4mbench dataset generator (4mdgen) simulates *food processing and packaging business* that is illustrated in Fig. 3. The business process is composed of nine procedures (P00 to P08), which manufacture final products (i.e., pallets storing cookie boxes) from raw materials (e.g., dough) [8,12]. The description of each procedure and its incoming and outgoing materials is summarized in Table 1.

The simulation is performed in a pseudo-event-driven manner; every time necessary incoming materials arrive, an operation unit of a procedure is immediately triggered and then produces an outgoing material after a specified latency on the simulation time[2]. For simplicity, sensor readings (e.g., dimensions and weight) of materials are independently determined according to Gaussian distribution with specified parameters. The operation unit fails at a specified rate. In the event of failure, no outgoing materials are produced.

4mdgen allows the user to specify two scale factors: the number of production lines $(N_L)$ and the number of business days $(N_D)$. For each day for each production line, 4mdgen simulates an eight-hour business operation of food processing and packaging to produce a dataset of manufacturing event records. Each production line is supposed to be independent, but the manufacturing business of a certain day takes over from that of the previous day. Roughly speaking, the dataset population is proportional to $N_L \times N_D$.

For benchmark simplicity, the simulation assumes that thirteen workers (W00 to W12) are assigned for the nine procedures in each production lines; only a worker is assigned for each procedure and its assignment rotates every day. Thus, four out of thirteen days are off for each worker.

Similarly, nine pieces of equipment (E00 to E08) are statically assigned for the nines procedures (P00 to P08) respectively in each production line. Equipment normality and a single sensor reading (e.g., equipment temperature) is produced every simulation second. These values are also determined according to Gaussian distribution with specified parameters. While a piece of equipment is not normal, an operation unit associated with the equipment is stalled.

## 3.3  Test Queries

4mbench specifies six test queries, which are summarized below. All these queries have been designed based on our business experience.

- **Production amount analysis (4mQ.1)** calculates the production amounts of MT04, MT06, MT08 and MT09 materials in each production line in each business hour on the most recent business day.
- **Equipment availability analysis (4mQ.2)** calculates the total equipment availability ratio of all the production lines on each business day for thirty days after a specified date [DATE].
- **Production lead time analysis (4mQ.3)** calculates the minimum, maximum and average values of production lead time in each production line on a specified date [DATE].
- **Quality test query (4mQ.4)** lists material IDs of all the defective MT04 materials that are packaged into the MT09 materials produced on a specific date [DATE] and have quality problems, material IDs of all the MT09 materials into which the defective MT04 materials are packaged, and the related production line IDs.

---

[2] Currently, the simulation is not fully event-driven. In reality, an operation unit may accept and process multiple materials at a time. But, the current implementation does not consider this parallelism for simplicity. Instead, we have opted to set smaller latency values (divided by the degree of parallelism) such that it can simulate the process parallelism approximately.

– **Equipment failure influence analysis (4mQ.5)** lists material IDs of all
  the materials which are packaged into any of defective MT04 materials, and
  material IDs of all the materials which package any of defective MT04 materials
  on a specific date [DATE].
– **Production yield analysis (4mQ.6)** calculates a production yield rate in
  each production line on a specific date [DATE].

Due to the space limitation, we would like to focus on a detailed definition
of **4mQ.3**, which is presented in Appendix A.1. This query contains a recursive
portion to trace the manufacturing operation history from final products (MT09)
to raw materials (MT00). This is distinctive to the manufacturing business process
since the production line is a chain of many operations. Similar queries have not
been necessarily actively experimented in performance studies. We expect that
our new benchmark will offer new findings.

## 4    Experimental Study

We performed intensive experiments to clarify how 4mbench effectively worked as
a performance benchmark of manufacturing business database. We ran 4mbench
on PostgreSQL 14.3 and experimentally studied the performance of loading and
query processing to explore the scope of further performance optimization.

All the experiments were conducted on a four-socket server HA8000V/DL380
Gen10 that had four Intel Xeon Gold 6240R (24 processing cores in each, with
hyperthreading enabled) and 768 GB memory with Red Hat Enterprise Linux
8.3. Two storage subsystems, Hitachi Virtual Storage Platform E790, were connected to the server via two 32 Gb Fibre Channel cables, exporting six storage
volumes in total; each volume was organized by seven 2.0 TB NVMe SSD modules in RAID-5. We bundled these six storage volumes with Linux LVM in a
striping manner into a single logical volume, in which an XFS file system was
built and PostgreSQL organized the database.

### 4.1    Dataset Generation and Loading

We ran 4mdgen to generate test datasets of the following different scales: small
($N_L = 3, N_D = 12$), middle ($N_L = 10, N_D = 40$) and large ($N_L = 30, N_D = 120$). Table 2 summarizes statistics of the generated datasets, indicating that the
size of each fact table (OPERATION_LOG, MATERIAL_LOG and EQUIPMENT_LOG) was
almost proportional to the scale configuration.

Table 3 presents a summary of material processing in the case of the middle
scale dataset. The processed amount of the MT04, MT06 and MT08 materials were
significantly smaller than their precedent materials. This was because the P03,
P05 and P07 procedures merged multiple incoming materials to produce outgoing
materials. There were other cases that the processed amount of materials was
slightly smaller than their precedent materials; for example, the number of MT01
was slightly smaller than the number of MT00. This was because several incoming

**Table 2.** Dataset statistics.

| | | Small scale | Middle scale | Large scale |
|---|---|---|---|---|
| Configuration | $N_L$ | 3 | 10 | 30 |
| | $N_D$ | 12 | 40 | 120 |
| # of records | WORKER | 39 | 130 | 390 |
| | EQUIPMENT | 27 | 90 | 270 |
| | PROCEDURE | 9 | 9 | 9 |
| | OPERATION_LOG | 34,681,228 | 385,348,846 | 3,468,151,048 |
| | MATERIAL_LOG | 46,836,154 | 520,404,745 | 4,683,660,142 |
| | EQUIPMENT_LOG | 20,995,740 | 233,285,490 | 2,099,566,926 |
| Total size in text files | | 11 GB | 115 GB | 1,086 GB |
| Total database size | | 24 GB | 271 GB | 2,441 GB |
| Loading time | | 333 s. | 3,536 s. | 41,842 s. |

**Table 3.** Material processing statistics (middle scale; $N_L = 10, N_D = 40$).

| Material # | Processed amount | Material # | Processed amount |
|---|---|---|---|
| MT00 | 114,851,550 | MT07 | 794,800 |
| MT01 | 114,738,757 | MT08 | 16,560 |
| MT02 | 114,738,757 | MT09 | 16,560 |
| MT03 | 114,736,722 | MT13 | 19,122,787 |
| MT04 | 19,122,787 | MT15 | 795,984 |
| MT05 | 19,103,616 | MT17 | 16,560 |
| MT06 | 795,984 | - | - |

materials were discarded due to the failure happening at an operation unit and several incoming materials stayed in the operation pipeline on the last day of the simulation.

With the database schema presented in Sect. 3.1, we configured three separate databases (each being associated with one of three dataset scales) on PostgreSQL and loaded each dataset using pg_bulkload command with LOADER=PARALLEL option. Table 2 summarizes statistics of the database loading; the database size and the loading time increased almost in proportion to the scale configuration. Note that, in configuring the schema, we set an index for each of the attribute sets that would appear in the selection and join predicates in the test queries[3]. Thus, the loading time included the index building time.

---

[3] The detailed index definition is disclosed at the source code repository [4].

## 4.2    Test Queries

We executed each of the six test queries (**4mQ.1** to **4mQ.6**) and measured the execution performance. A place holder [DATE] was substituted by a date value randomly chosen value among the valid business dates[4] . Appendix A.2 summarizes the date values that we employed in the experiment. This measurement was performed for the three (small, middle and large) datasets and it was conducted strictly under the cold start condition; on each trial, the cache memory of the storage controller and the page cache of the Linux kernel were cleared, and the PostgreSQL process was restarted. In this experiment, PostgreSQL was configured with our tuning knowledge to minimize the execution time on the large dataset, and the database statistics were collected after the database loading. Appendix A.3 summarizes the configuration parameters that we changed.

Figure 4 presents how the execution performance changed on different queries and different dataset scales. Figure 4(a) summarizes the execution time of the six test queries. Note that the vertical axis is logarithmic. The execution time significantly varied among the test queries, but it mostly increased as the dataset scale grew up. Figure 4(b) summarizes the relative execution time, which is normalized on the basis of the small case. This chart indicates that the sensitivity of the query execution performance on the dataset scale is not necessarily consistent among the test queries; **4mQ.1** and **4mQ.6** had lower sensitivities than the proportionality, whereas **4mQ.3** and **4mQ.5** had higher sensitivities.

We investigated what was behind the high sensitivity of **4mQ.3**, because this query is typical to the manufacturing business as described in Sect. 3.3. Figure 5 summarizes query execution plans that were chosen by PostgreSQL for executing **4mQ.3** on different dataset scales. The hash join algorithm was chosen for the join operation between the recursive subquery part and MATERIAL_LOG on the small dataset, while the merge join algorithm was chosen for the same join operation on the middle and large datasets. The difference in join algorithms seemed to cause a significant extension of execution time.

## 4.3    4mQ.3 on Different Settings

We further studied the capability of PostgreSQL by running the test query **4mQ.3** with different settings. The previous experiment was performed after the database statistics were fully collected. Here, we tested the opposite case; specifically, the database statistics were not collected. In addition, we attempted the hinting phrase /*+ NestLoop(R M) Leading(R M) */ to instruct PostgreSQL to employ the nested-loop join algorithm for the join operation between the recursive subquery part (R) and MATERIAL_LOG (M). This is because that the previous experiment confirmed that PostgreSQL chose the hash join or merge join algorithms on the same join operation.

---

[4] The choice of the date may affect the query workload amount of **m4Q.2**. Thus, this paper does not deep dive into the performance comparison between different dataset scales for **m4Q.2**.

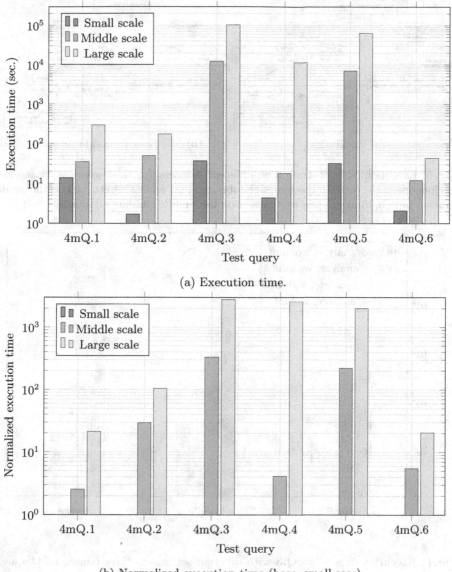

(a) Execution time.

(b) Normalized execution time (base: small case).

**Fig. 4.** Execution time of six test queries (**4mQ.1** to **4mQ.6**) in three (small, middle and large) scales. Execution time significantly varied among the test queries, and increased as the dataset scale grew, but the sensitivity also significantly varied.

Figure 6 presents the result, confirming that the database statistics did not consistently succeed in performance optimization, but the nested-loop join algorithm (instructed by the hinting phrase) significantly reduced the execution

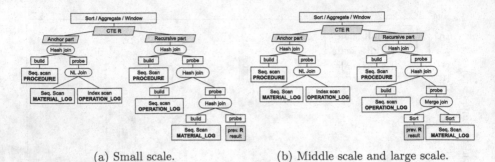

(a) Small scale.                    (b) Middle scale and large scale.

**Fig. 5.** Execution plans of **4mQ.3** on different datasets. (a) Hash join was chosen for the join operation between the recursive subquery part and `MATERIAL_LOG` on the small dataset, but (b, c) merge join was chosen on the middle and large datasets.

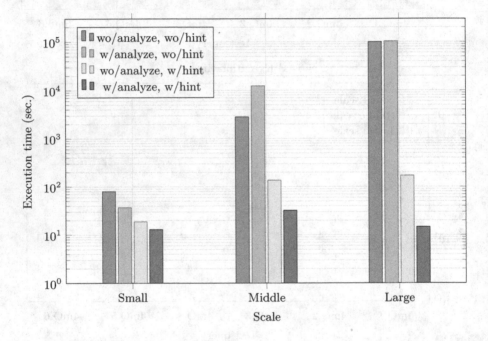

**Fig. 6.** Execution time of **4mQ.3** with different settings in three (small, middle and large) dataset scales.

time. **wo/analyze** and **w/analyze** indicate that the database statistics were not collected, and that the database statistics were fully collected. **wo/hint** and **w/hint** indicate that the test query was given without any hinting phrase, and that the test query was given with a hinting phrase which instructed the nested-loop join algorithm.

The findings can be summarized below. First, let us look into the blue and red bars, in which PostgreSQL fully controlled the query optimization. The use

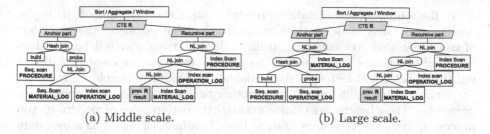

(a) Middle scale.                                    (b) Large scale.

**Fig. 7.** Execution plans of **4mQ.3** with a hinting phrase.

of database statistics successfully reduced the execution time to 46.4% on the small dataset, but it rather extended the execution time up to 434% on the middle dataset. Second, let us note the brown and gray bars, in which the hinting phrase forced the nested-loop join algorithm. Interestingly, this option succeeded to reduce the execution time consistently. The reduction reached up to an order of magnitude on the small dataset, and even up to four orders of magnitude on the large dataset. Third, the gray bar indicated that the execution time was shorter on the large dataset than on the middle dataset. In order to understand this curious phenomenon, we investigated query execution plans in both cases, which are illustrated in Fig. 7. The plan of the anchor part in the test query changed between the two cases, implying that, even with the hinting phrase, the query execution plan on the middle dataset could be further improved.

In summary, these experiments that we conducted with 4mbench have indicated that the existing query optimization may yield detrimental query execution plans, offering significantly (up to four orders of magnitude) longer execution time for manufacturing business questions. We hope that 4mbench provides researchers and developers with opportunities to explore the scope of further performance optimization on manufacturing business database.

## 5   Related Work

In the past, the "one size fits all" strategy was popular in the database system market, but today this concept is no longer valid [16]. The variety of applications handled by database systems has become significantly wider than they were a few decades ago, and the approach of tailoring database systems to meet various business applications is becoming the norm. Benchmarks are the most important measure for evaluating such database systems [5].

Traditionally, database benchmarks have two main categories: transactional processing and analytical processing. There are several well-known benchmarks: TPC-C [18] and TPC-E [19] are for transaction processing; TPC-H [20], TPC-DS [13] and Star Schema Benchmark [14] for analytical processing. As a new way of using database systems has emerged, a new benchmark has also emerged accordingly such as TPC-W [11] for web commerce and ESQUE [6] for event sequence analysis.

In the context of sensor data processing, Linear Road benchmark [1] is pioneering work. It is modeled after an application that estimates the likelihood of congestion and accidents from traffic volumes at highway toll booths. Linear Road benchmark mainly focuses on continuous stream processing of incoming traffic data, and historical data analysis is limited to simple aggregation. StreamBench [10] and Senska [7] are another benchmarks assuming sensor data processing. These benchmarks aim to evaluate the performance of modern stream processing systems. As we have stated above, benchmarks regarding sensor data processing are primarily interested in the performance of stream data processing. Performance benchmarking of complex decision support queries in the manufacturing business has not been investigated as far as we know in the literature.

## 6    Conclusion

This paper has presented *4mbench*, a performance benchmark for decision support database in the manufacturing business. 4mbench has employed the 4m (man, machine, material and method) model in order to organize manufacturing event records into relational database and allow business questions to be queried on those event records. This paper has described the overall design of the benchmark that assumes business operation of food processing and packaging and presented an experimental case study that we conducted with 4mbench on PostgreSQL. This experiment suggested that the existing query optimization might yield detrimental query execution plans, offering significantly (up to four orders of magnitude) longer execution time. We hope that 4mbench provides researchers and developers with opportunities to explore the scope of further performance optimization on manufacturing business database.

## Artifact Availability

The source code of 4mbench is disclosed at the public repository [4].

**Acknowledgements.** This work has been in part supported by "Big Data Value Co-creation Platform Engineering" social cooperation program at Institute of Industrial Science, The University of Tokyo with Hitachi, Ltd.

## A    Experiment Configuration

### A.1    SQL Description of Test Query (4mQ.3)

```
WITH RECURSIVE R (ML_LID, ML_MLID_MT09, WORK_NAME, ML_MLID, ML_MTYPE,
            ML_OLID_SRC, ML_OLID_DST, OL_TSBEGIN, OL_TSEND) AS (
  SELECT ML_LID, ML_MLID,
         CASE WHEN OL_PID IN (8, 7, 6) THEN 'W03' ELSE
           CASE WHEN OL_PID IN (5, 4) THEN 'W02' ELSE
             CASE WHEN OL_PID IN (3, 2, 1, 0) THEN 'W01' END
           END
         END
```

```
          END,
          ML_MLID, ML_MTYPE, ML_OLID_SRC, ML_OLID_DST,
          OL_TSBEGIN, OL_TSEND
    FROM MATERIAL_LOG, OPERATION_LOG, PROCEDURE
    WHERE ML_LID=OL_LID AND ML_OLID_SRC=OL_OLID AND OL_PID=P_PID
          AND OL_TSEND BETWEEN DATE'[DATE]' AND
                              DATE'[DATE]' + INTERVAL '1 DAY'
          AND OL_LID = 109 AND P_PNAME='PROCEDURE000008 (STORAGING)'
    UNION ALL
    SELECT R.ML_LID, R.ML_MLID_MT09,
          CASE WHEN O.OL_PID IN (8, 7, 6) THEN 'W03' ELSE
            CASE WHEN O.OL_PID IN (5, 4) THEN 'W02' ELSE
              CASE WHEN O.OL_PID IN (3, 2, 1, 0) THEN 'W01' END
            END
          END,
          M.ML_MLID, M.ML_MTYPE, M.ML_OLID_SRC, M.ML_OLID_DST,
          O.OL_TSBEGIN, O.OL_TSEND
    FROM R, MATERIAL_LOG M, OPERATION_LOG O, PROCEDURE P
    WHERE R.ML_LID = M.ML_LID AND R.ML_OLID_SRC = M.ML_OLID_DST
          AND M.ML_MTYPE IN ('MT08', 'MT07', 'MT06', 'MT05', 'MT04',
                            'MT03', 'MT02', 'MT01', 'MT00')
      AND M.ML_LID=O.OL_LID AND M.ML_OLID_SRC=O.OL_OLID
      AND O.OL_PID=P.P_PID
)
SELECT ML_LID, HR, WORK_NAME,
      MAX(LEADTIME), MIN(LEADTIME), AVG(LEADTIME), SUM(CNT)
FROM (
  SELECT ML_LID, ML_MLID_MT09, WORK_NAME, HR,
          W_TSEND - W_TSBEGIN AS LEADTIME, COUNT(*) AS CNT
  FROM (
    SELECT ML_LID, ML_MLID_MT09, WORK_NAME,
            MIN(OL_TSBEGIN)
              OVER (PARTITION BY ML_LID, ML_MLID_MT09, WORK_NAME)
              AS W_TSBEGIN,
            MAX(OL_TSEND)
              OVER (PARTITION BY ML_LID, ML_MLID_MT09, WORK_NAME)
              AS W_TSEND,
            DATE_TRUNC('HOUR', OL_TSEND) AS HR
    FROM R
  ) A
  GROUP BY ML_LID, ML_MLID_MT09, HR, WORK_NAME, W_TSEND - W_TSBEGIN
) B
GROUP BY ML_LID, HR, WORK_NAME
ORDER BY HR, WORK_NAME;
```

## A.2    [DATE] Variable Substitution

| Dataset | 4mQ2 | 4mQ3 | 4mQ4 | 4mQ5 | 4mQ6 |
|---|---|---|---|---|---|
| Small scale | 2022-04-10 | 2022-04-01 | 2022-04-08 | 2022-04-03 | 2022-04-06 |
| Middle scale | 2022-04-15 | 2022-04-29 | 2022-04-22 | 2022-04-15 | 2022-04-15 |
| Large scale | 2022-04-25 | 2022-06-22 | 2022-06-20 | 2022-07-28 | 2022-07-03 |

## A.3    Configuration Parameters of PostgreSQL

| Parameter | Default value | Tuned value |
|---|---|---|
| max_connections | 100 | 10 |
| shared_buffers | 128 MB | 16 GB |
| temp_buffers | 8 MB | 16 GB |
| work_mem | 4 MB | 16 GB |
| maintenance_work_mem | 64 MB | 16 GB |
| effectiv_io_concurrency | 1 | 256 |
| maintenance_io_concurrency | 10 | 128 |
| max_worker_processes | 8 | 48 |
| max_parallel_workers_per_gather | 2 | 24 |
| max_parallel_workers | 8 | 24 |

# References

1. Arasu, A., et al.: Linear road: a stream data management benchmark. In: VLDB, pp. 480–491. Morgan Kaufmann (2004)
2. Bradley, E.: Reliability Engineering: A Life Cycle Approach. CRC Press (2016)
3. Favi, C., Germani, M., Marconi, M.: A 4M approach for a comprehensive analysis and improvement of manual assembly lines. Procedia Manufact. **11**, 1510–1518 (2017)
4. Goda, K., Hayamizu, Y.: 4mbench: a tool for performance benchmark of manufacturing business database. https://www.github.com/dbc-utokyoiis/4mbench/
5. Gray, J.: A "measure of transaction processing" 20 years later. IEEE Data Eng. Bull. **28**(2), 3–4 (2005)
6. Hayamizu, Y., Kawamichi, R., Goda, K., Kitsuregawa, M.: Benchmarking and performance analysis of event sequence queries on relational database. In: Nambiar, R., Poess, M. (eds.) TPCTC 2018. LNCS, vol. 11135, pp. 110–125. Springer, Cham (2019). https://doi.org/10.1007/978-3-030-11404-6_9
7. Hesse, G., Reissaus, B., Matthies, C., Lorenz, M., Kraus, M., Uflacker, M.: Senska – towards an enterprise streaming benchmark. In: Nambiar, R., Poess, M. (eds.) TPCTC 2017. LNCS, vol. 10661, pp. 25–40. Springer, Cham (2018). https://doi.org/10.1007/978-3-319-72401-0_3

8. Kinchla, A., Richards, N., Pivarnik, L.: Food safety plan for chocolate chip cookie teaching example. https://ag.umass.edu/sites/ag.umass.edu/files/cookiefoodsafetyplan.pdf. Accessed 19 June 19
9. Lin, Y.C., et al.: Development of advanced manufacturing cloud of things (AMCoT)-a smart manufacturing platform. IEEE Robot. Autom. Lett. **2**(3), 1809–1816 (2017)
10. Lu, R., Wu, G., Xie, B., Hu, J.: Stream bench: towards benchmarking modern distributed stream computing frameworks. In: UCC, pp. 69–78. IEEE Computer Society (2014)
11. Menascé, D.A.: TPC-W: a benchmark for e-commerce. IEEE Internet Comput. **6**(3), 83–87 (2002)
12. Ministry of Health, British Columbia: Food Safety Plan Workbook. https://www2.gov.bc.ca/assets/gov/health/keeping-bc-healthy-safe/food-safety-security/food_safety_plan_workbook_sept6_2017.pdf. Accessed 19 June 2022
13. Nambiar, R.O., Poess, M.: The making of TPC-DS. In: VLDB, pp. 1049–1058. ACM (2006)
14. O'Neil, P., O'Neil, E., Chen, X., Revilak, S.: The star schema benchmark and augmented fact table indexing. In: Nambiar, R., Poess, M. (eds.) TPCTC 2009. LNCS, vol. 5895, pp. 237–252. Springer, Heidelberg (2009). https://doi.org/10.1007/978-3-642-10424-4_17
15. O'Donovan, P., Leahy, K., Bruton, K., O'Sullivan, D.T.J.: An industrial big data pipeline for data-driven analytics maintenance applications in large-scale smart manufacturing facilities. J. Big Data **2**(1), 1–26 (2015). https://doi.org/10.1186/s40537-015-0034-z
16. Stonebraker, M., Çetintemel, U.: "One size fits all": an idea whose time has come and gone. In: Making Databases Work, pp. 441–462. ACM/Morgan & Claypool (2019)
17. Tao, F., Qi, Q., Liu, A., Kusiak, A.: Data-driven smart manufacturing. J. Manuf. Syst. **48**, 157–169 (2018)
18. Transaction Processing Performance Council: TPC-C benchmark specification. https://www.tpc.org/tpcc/
19. Transaction Processing Performance Council: TPC-E benchmark specification. https://www.tpc.org/tpce/
20. Transaction Processing Performance Council: TPC-H benchmark specification. https://www.tpc.org/tpch/
21. Wang, S., Wan, J., Li, D., Zhang, C.: Implementing smart factory of industrie 4.0: an outlook. Int. J. Distrib. Sens. Netw. **12**(1), 3159805 (2016)
22. Weeden, M.M.: Failure Mode and Effects Analysis (FMEAs) for Small Business Owners and Non-engineers: Determining and Preventing What Can Go Wrong. ASQ Quality Press (2015)
23. Yang, H., Kumara, S., Bukkapatnam, S.T., Tsung, F.: The internet of things for smart manufacturing: a review. IISE Trans. **51**(11), 1190–1216 (2019)

# Benchmarking Considerations for Trustworthy and Responsible AI (Panel)

Ajay Dholakia[1]([⊠]), David Ellison[1], Miro Hodak[2], and Debojyoti Dutta[3]

[1] Lenovo, Infrastructure Solutions Group, Morrisville, NC, USA
`{adholakia,dellison}@lenovo.com`
[2] AMD, San Jose, CA, USA
`Miro.Hodak@amd.com`
[3] Nutanix, San Jose, CA, USA
`debojyoti.dutta@nutanix.com`

**Abstract.** Continuing growth of Artificial Intelligence (AI) adoption across enterprises and governments around the world has fueled the demand for trustworthy AI systems and applications. The need ranges from the so-called Explainable or Interpretable AI to Responsible AI, driven by the underlying demand for increasing confidence in deploying AI as part of Enterprise IT. Both internal to organizations as well as external, customer- and user-facing use cases based on AI are increasingly being expected to meet these demands. This paper describes the need for and definitions of trustworthiness and responsibility in AI systems, summarizes currently popular AI benchmarks, and deliberates on the challenges and the opportunities for assessing and benchmarking Trustworthy and Responsible aspects of AI systems and applications.

**Keywords:** Artificial Intelligence · Benchmarks · Trustworthy · Responsible · Explainable · Interpretable

## 1 Introduction

AI-enabled systems are now in active use across a host of personal and commercial applications. The past decade has seen continuous growth in the adoption of AI across enterprises and governmental organizations. The ensuing benefits are expected to prompt even faster adoption in the coming decade and beyond. Alongside this growth in AI systems, industry and academia have focused on developing benchmarks for evaluating and comparing AI systems [1]. Currently the MLPerf benchmark [2–4], created by the MLCommons organization, is very popular, driven by a sizeable community of technology leaders in AI and a regular cadence of releases with dozens of submitters. The recent release of TPCx-AI [5, 6] in August 2021 has broadened the scope of benchmarking activities focused on AI workloads.

With the growth of AI systems, and especially applications of Foundation Models [7], has come the need and demand for increasing trust and responsibility in these systems. Humans are direct or indirect users of AI-enabled systems and the impact of adopting

R. Nambiar and M. Poess (Eds.): TPCTC 2022, LNCS 13860, pp. 110–119, 2023.
https://doi.org/10.1007/978-3-031-29576-8_8

recommendations or decisions made by AI systems can be far reaching. Disciplines like medicine, healthcare, law and governance, financial systems and services, manufacturing and so on require decisions affecting end-users to be understandable, interpretable, dependable and auditable. This has spawned an entirely new domain of research and development called Explainable AI (XAI). The XAI community is exploring answers to questions like "Can the AI model prediction be explained?" and "How good is the explanation?", to state just a few. Conceptually, it is not difficult to take the next step and ask about measuring the goodness of explanations of AI model outputs. This, then brings up the question of extending benchmarks for AI systems to include aspects like trust and responsibility.

The goal of this work is to examine the notions of trustworthiness and responsibility in AI systems and tease out metrics that will eventually enable measurements and benchmarking. One would like to pose questions like "Which explanation is better?" and "Which AI system is more trustworthy?" and even "How responsible is an AI system?" These are difficult questions and the research in this area is in its infancy. Therefore, we attempt here to merely pose the questions and provide the associated definitions of component constructs that often make up meta-concepts like trust and responsibility. We also discuss examples of metrics from recent literature that can be employed for measuring these nebulous characteristics.

We would like to emphasize that we look at trustworthiness and responsibility through the lens of benchmarking. In that context, these terms may take on a new meaning. For instance, a responsible benchmark may be thought of as a performance measurement that takes into account other factors that are important to the society beyond just the performance. For example, creating efficiency metrics, such as performance per watt or per cost, is a way to make benchmarking more responsible.

Another way the benchmarking community can help address the need for more trustworthiness and responsibility is that it can develop automated tools that would evaluate those properties in AI models.

This paper is organized as follows: Sect. 2 summarizes MLPerf and TPCx-AI benchmarks, pointing out accuracy as a basic "trust" metric and "power efficiency" as a "responsible" metric. Section 3 provides definitions related to trust and responsibility in AI and cites recent literature. Section 4 provides recent examples of work extending the accuracy and power efficiency metrics, to address XAI, including human-in-the-loop and other approaches. Section 5 discusses the evolutionary as well as revolutionary opportunities in developing metrics and benchmarks for trustworthy and responsible AI and calls out challenges that need to be overcome. Finally, Sect. 6 restates the position of this paper and lays out areas of ongoing and future work.

## 2 Current State of AI Benchmarking

AI benchmarking work in industry as well as academia has been ramping up over the past few years. While performance evaluation of AI workloads has been an active area of research, benchmark development has been a more recent trend. A survey of AI benchmarking work in industry as well as academia has been ramping up over the past few years. Recently, MLPerf [2–4] has emerged as the leading AI benchmarking tool.

MLPerf is developed by MLCommons, a consortium dedicated to advancement of AI, which has some of the leading AI leading companies as members. MLPerf publishes separate benchmarks for Inference and Training stages of AI workflow.

Previous works [8, 9] by some of the authors have reviewed the MLPerf benchmark and its results in some depth. In particular, we have pointed out that there was no efficiency metric, as the best results were always achieved by the largest computer systems – by the most scale-out system in training or by the servers that contained most accelerators in the case of inference.

This has changed very recently: The version 1.0 release of Inference, released in April 2021, included a power metric, which reports power used while performing inference. This is a very welcome change, but it does not go far enough: Power results are reported in a separate spreadsheet and their number is very small compared to the main results. The most recent Inference release, version 2.1, has 9 power entries compared 70 results in the main Closed division. Another issue is that power results are often run in a power-efficient way sacrificing efficiency. For example, one power entry (Nvidia A100 ResNet50 Inference) only achieves about 80% of performance compared to the results where power was not tracked. While this is still valuable, it ultimately fails in conveying how much power is used to achieve the most performant results.

We should also acknowledge that adding a power measurement introduces a substantial burden on submitters – an approved and calibrated power meter needs to be used, which requires significant expertise. This is the most likely reason for a low adoption of the metric. Nevertheless, the results have been very valuable and have provided some of the only peer-reviewed data for power usage in AI tasks.

One way to improve the situation would be to use a metric that does not require a separate measurement. DawnBench [10], an MLPerf predecessor, used a cost incurred by using public instances as a way to evaluate training cost. Or, power cost can be estimated for results where it was not measured by using TDP – Thermal Design Power – which expresses the amount of thermal energy in Watts that needs to be dissipated for a given compute chip. Admittedly, this would be much less accurate than measurement, but it would force submitters to pay more attention to power efficiency.

A different approach to AI benchmarking and efficiency is being taken by TPCx-AI [5, 6]. Released about a year ago, this benchmark attempts to evaluate the end-to-end AI workload instead of treating Training and Inference separately. In addition to those two stages, TPCx-AI includes data handling tasks and its workflow mimics AI tasks used in a retail environment. In terms of efficiency, it includes a cost-based metric, which is easier to evaluate because it does not require a separate setup and measurement.

## 3   Deconstructing Trust and Responsibility in AI

Defining terms such as trust and responsibility in relation to AI systems requires breaking them down into components to enable clearer descriptions. For example, trust in a system can be based on fairness, quality, auditability, provenance, reproducibility and replicability. Similarly, responsible systems encompass requirements spanning efficient resource consumption, equitable usage and fairness. Furthermore, the ability to interpret and explain predictions and recommendations made by an AI system underlies trust and responsibility. Therefore, it is necessary to deconstruct these concepts into components that can be identified, measured, and compared.

Explainable AI (XAI) has become a topic of very active research. A recent survey [11] of XAI research included over 425 articles. This body of research undoubtedly will continue to grow significantly. The authors in [11] make the argument that increasing use of the so-called "black box" machine learning models in critical contexts such as medicine, law, and defense has increased the demand for transparency from key users and stakeholders in AI. Interpretability is becoming a foundational concept in XAI by facilitating a level of impartiality in decision-making as well as robustness against adversarial perturbations.

Taking a similar deconstruction approach, [12] curated a set of papers that examined XAI by separating and studying interpretability, reproducibility and replicability. In defining these terms, the authors in [12] follow the guidelines from the US National Academies [13]. Reproducibility is the ability to obtain consistent results using the same data and code as the original study. Replicability is obtaining consistency using new data or methods in studies aiming to answer the same scientific question.

Trustworthiness of AI systems can then be based on interpretability, reproducibility and replicability. In addition, trust may involve transparent knowledge of the data and model provenance in the sense of guaranteeing fair and robust outcomes.

Responsible AI goes beyond trustworthiness by requiring factors such as avoiding adverse effects from use of AI systems for critical decision making. The scope of such effects may include avoidance of harm to the user, social responsibility, equitability and efficient use of physical resources [11].

Many definitions of Responsible AI have been developed by various organizations [14–16]. For the purposes of this paper, we will explore the framework set forth by the European Commission [14]. In this framework, the following requirements are enumerated:

1. Human Agency and Oversight
2. Technical Robustness and Safety
3. Privacy and Data Governance
4. Transparency
5. Diversity, Non-discrimination and Fairness
6. Societal and Environmental Well-being
7. Accountability

The first principle is Human Agency and Oversight which means that AI systems should support human decision-making and respect human autonomy. AI systems should uphold fundamental rights and have sufficient human oversight. This includes the effect AI systems can have on human behavior and the effects AI can have when influencing or supporting humans in making decisions. This can happen in a wide variety of settings from credit risk, to medical decision making, to predictive policing to name a few. It includes the effect AI systems can have on humans when the user is perhaps unclear on whether he is interacting with an AI system. Finally, it involves human oversight on the capability for human intervention in every decision cycle of the system.

Requirement two is Technical Robustness and Safety. This requires systems to deliver services that can be trusted and are robust to changes in input and against attacks. This robustness prescribes that AI systems be developed to ward proactively against risks and mitigate or eliminate unintentional harms. It includes security against adversarial attacks and cybersecurity attacks. This is especially important in AI since there are additional vulnerabilities in AI systems of data poisoning (manipulating training data to corrupt the model), model evasion (manipulating the environment to classify data according to the attacker's wishes), and model inversion (attacks which extract model parameters or training data). Finally reliability is a part of this requirement since it is desired for a system to monitor its decisions to ensure it is continuing to give accurate results.

Privacy and Data Governance are the third requirement in this framework. Privacy is a fundamental right that is especially affected by AI systems. Systems should closely self-assess how the AI could impact privacy. Data privacy extends to both the training data used to make the models and the data that the trained model runs on which is the inference data. If the model is trained on data that does not respect the privacy and/or has the consent of the subjects it can make the model problematic to use even if the inference stage protects the privacy of the subjects. Data Governance also has to be addressed since the data needs to be well-managed or there can be significant risks associated with the system.

Transparency is the fourth requirement and encompasses traceability, explainability, and open communication about the limits of the AI system. Traceability is the process by which the AI system's decisions are properly documented. This allows a user to see what data and models were used to come to a particular decision. Keeping track of this information can be especially difficult in AI systems where data sizes are hard to store and models are continually updated. A large part of transparency is explainability which refers to the ability to reveal the reasoning behind the predictions that the AI system made. For example in the case of credit risk, a potential borrower might want to know the specific reasons his loan was denied. However an explanation as to how a model comes to decision is not always possible – these cases are referred to as 'black boxes'. In the case of black boxes many model-independent algorithms have been developed to help understand which inputs or factors may have caused a decision to be made even if that information cannot be extracted from the model itself. Finally open communication about the limitations of the AI system is important for the user to know both if he is interacting with an AI system instead of a human and if he is interacting with an AI system, how much he should rely on the predictions the system makes.

Diversity, Non-discrimination and Fairness is the fifth requirement for responsible AI. Diversity and inclusion must be a central part of the lifecycle of an AI system. Bias can creep in through many different pathways, but a primary concern is via the training data. The training data can include inadvertent historic bias, incomplete or non-balanced data, or simply be poorly collected data. Specifically on non-balanced data it is often difficult and requires special attention to acquire data belonging to minority groups. Without sufficient examples of each minority group, the trained model can essentially 'overlook' those data and/or combine it with unrelated data. Additionally, AI systems should be designed in such a way that people with diverse backgrounds and abilities can successfully use the product.

Requirement number six is Societal and Environmental Well-being. For this require-ment the broader society and environment need to be protected from harm and ideally helped by AI systems. The effects of AI must be monitored and studied throughout its lifecycle. An example of this could be the impact of Social Media on personal happiness and the polarization of democracies. These impacts should be mitigated and prevented where possible, or at least balanced with positive aspects of the AI system. Sustainability is also an important area of AI – balancing AI's impact today with the needs of future generations. This becomes especially important as particularly large language models and other very large deep learning models can require tremendous amounts of energy to train. The benefit of the system now must be balanced with the $CO_2$ emissions that creating the model takes.

The final requirement is Accountability. There should be mechanism and processes set up that ensure there is a human responsible for the use of AI systems. Third parties should be able to audit the AI system and assign responsibility for the harm caused by their use. When harm is caused, there should be means established to ensure redress by the parties harmed.

These seven requirements cover AI and AI systems is a broad way. There are many ways in which to divide and define the requirements of AI systems however these seven requirements provide a strong basis from which to define responsible AI.

# 4 Metrics for Trust and Responsibility

The definitions and taxonomy from the previous section enable formulation of metrics to capture quantitative measures associated with them. This will, in turn, enable comparison across AI systems and help formulate relevant benchmarking criteria and toolkits.

Existing AI benchmarks described in a previous section use metrics such as accuracy to measure and compare AI systems. It is easy to argue that an AI system that is more accurate is more trustworthy. More recently, the popular AI benchmarks have added efficiency metrics like accuracy and throughput per unit of cost or per unit of power. The idea of measuring such resource usage efficiency is indeed a step towards responsible AI. These are, therefore, initial steps that allow basic characterization of the trust and responsibility aspects of AI systems. However, trust and responsibility are highly com-plex concepts and must be examined thoroughly from various perspectives to arrive at an understanding that defines measurable metrics and can promote wider adoption.

Examples of quantitative measures and metrics related to XAI are not easily available. One approach taken in [17] is to focus on post hoc gradient-based local methods in XAI to enumerate a set of metrics such as fidelity, sensitively, sanity checks, perturbation-based evaluation as well as evaluation using remove and retrain (ROAR) process. The collective goal is to answer the question "How good is an explanation?" and the associated approaches aim to attribute the impact of specific features on the ML model outputs. The metrics mentioned above are still in early stages of research and evaluation and come with a host of limitations. A key limitation stems from the inability to separate errors in attribution to those made by the models from those made by the attribution methods.

The role of humans in the loop for obtaining explanations is very useful. In particular, ML models used in Computer Vision systems can benefit from humans evaluating and interpreting the model outputs. At the minimum, a passing criterion can be used to accept or reject the model output based on human interpretation. However, human bias may become a factor rather than the mechanics of how the model arrived at a decision.

A recent work combines machine and human agents in a multi-agent system to improve ML model trustworthiness [18]. Their approach is to calculate a trust score based on initial values of the system, e.g., the current model, the training set and the training code. The trust score is then used to identify anomalous instances which are then modified through human agent assistance and used in a transfer learning step to improve the trustworthiness.

For classification tasks, [19] have developed a so-called "Trust Score" as a quantitative measure of trust. This is different from the confidence or related measures typically provided by a classifier. The Trust Score is defined as the ratio between the distance from the testing sample to the nearest class different from the predicted class and the distance to the predicted class. This metric can be used to determine whether to trust that classifier prediction. The authors in [19] show empirically that their metric outperforms the classifiers' own reported confidence in identifying trustworthy and suspicious examples across a range of datasets and classifiers.

Metrics go beyond definitions of component concepts that make up trust and responsibility. One needs to be able to measure the extent of reproducibility or replicability. Similarly, one needs to ascertain provenance of datasets used in training models. The explanations about results predicted by AI systems may not be absolute and may allow relative comparison among a number of possible explanations. In all these cases, it might make sense to come up with a quantitative measure that captures the components of the property being examined. If such a measure can then be systematically determined for different AI systems that are designed to address a common use case, comparison between systems will become possible. This can then lead to the definition of a benchmarking procedure for the property in consideration.

## 5   Challenges and Opportunities for Benchmarking Trust and Interpretability

The discussion of various aspects of trust and responsibility in the context of AI systems and the associated formulation of metrics in the preceding sections has made it evident that these are not simple problems to solve. While having metrics to measure such capabilities of a given AI system is highly desirable, there are significant challenges in achieving these goals. In this section, we discuss a range of challenges that lie ahead as we take this journey to create benchmarks for such meta concepts.

In developing a benchmark, we need to refine the questions of the type "How good is an explanation?" to ones like "Which explanation is better?" and "Which method and metric generates a better explanation?" That is, the goal is to enable relative comparison between methods applied to a target system, or the same method running on different systems.

On the challenges front, we must consider some inherent conflicts in developing metrics. For instance, are XAI and Responsible AI at odds with each other? If it is "responsible" to conserve energy, but use of XAI methods requires additional energy

consumption, then is it irresponsible to implement XAI? The trade-off pits energy efficiency against increase in trust based on explanations. What are some ways to resolve
this and other similar conflicts that may arise in practical implementations?

These are going to be some of the key challenges that the AI community needs to
resolve. Given the nature of such problems, it will require participation from experts
in many related fields, including some that are decidedly outside the domain of AI, to
arrive at metrics and benchmarks that are meaningful to the society at large.

On the opportunities front, two possible approaches are emerging. These can be
broadly categorized as evolutionary and revolutionary. Evolutionary approach is focused
on extending existing benchmarks by modifying currently used metrics and adding new
ones to address notions of trust and responsibility. There are two aspects of an AI
system: datasets and models. Most enterprise AI teams often re-tune standard models
for their purpose. For example, a customer contact center application often re-tunes a
large language/foundation model, e.g., BERT [20] or GPT-2 [21], for its applications like
a chatbot. An extension can start with the BERT model and define metrics for privacy,
safety and explainability. In the case of BERT, explainability can be understood via
attention metrics. There are aspects like faithfulness of explanations evaluating closeness
of the explanation to the inner workings of the model [22] and plausibility in the sense of
a user accepting the explanation as plausible [23]. However, the use of attention metrics
in XAI is a topic of current research [7, 24] and positions it as an ongoing debate.

The revolutionary approach will need to consider the meta-concepts of trust and
responsibility in total and aim to formulate metrics that enable measurements at the highest conceptual levels. These will require examining component concepts as described
earlier in this paper. Each of these component concepts may be measurable individually,
and a lot of current research is focusing in this area. However, the component measures
will then need to be combined to arrive at a top-level score which will in turn enable
development of a benchmark.

Opportunities for defining use metrics for a range of concepts related to trustworthiness and responsibility in AI may come from targeting specific aspects of the end-to-end
AI workflow. As done in the TPCx-AI benchmark, the AI workflow is made of multiple
stages, from data acquisition, to data processing including cleaning and integration, to
dataset creation, to model training and evaluation to model serving. Each state can be a
focus of incorporating aspects of trust and responsibility.

## 6  Summary and Conclusions

This paper focused on articulating the need for developing benchmarks for trust and
interpretability aspects of AI systems. Currently popular benchmarks for AI systems
use metrics such as accuracy and throughput and also require measurement of these
performance metrics per unit of cost or per unit of power. These are indeed necessary
steps in gaining trust in and increasing the responsibility shown by AI systems. However,
significantly more work is needed to develop, debate, agree on and select metrics and
benchmarks that enable AI systems to demonstrate trustworthiness and responsibility.

# References

1. Bourrasset, C., et al.: Requirements for an enterprise AI benchmark. In: Nambiar, R., Poess, M. (eds.) TPCTC 2018. LNCS, vol. 11135, pp. 71–81. Springer, Cham (2019). https://doi.org/10.1007/978-3-030-11404-6_6
2. MLPerf. https://mlcommons.org/
3. Mattson, P., et al.: MLPerf training benchmark. Proc. Mach. Learn. Syst. **2**, 336–349 (2020)
4. Reddy, V.J., et al.: MLPerf Inference Benchmark. arXiv preprint arXiv: 1911:02549 (2019)
5. TPCx-AI. https://www.tpc.org/tpcx-ai/default5.asp.
6. Transaction Processing and Performance Council, "TPC Express Benchmark ™ AI - Full Disclosure Report" (2022)
7. Bommasani, R., et. al.: On the opportunities and risks of foundation models. arXiv preprint https://arxiv.org/pdf/2108.07258.pdf. (2022)
8. Hodak, M., Ellison, D., Dholakia, A.: Benchmarking AI inference: where we are in 2020. In: Nambiar, R., Poess, M. (eds.) TPCTC 2020. LNCS, vol. 12752, pp. 93–102. Springer, Cham (2021). https://doi.org/10.1007/978-3-030-84924-5_7
9. Hodak, M., Ellison, D., Dholakia, A.: Everyone is a winner: interpreting MLPerf inference benchmark results. In: Nambiar, R., Poess, M. (eds.) TPCTC 2021. LNCS, vol. 13169, pp. 50–61. Springer, Cham (2022). https://doi.org/10.1007/978-3-030-94437-7_4
10. Coleman, C.A., et al.: DAWNBench: an end-to-end deep learning benchmark and competition. In: Proceedings of the 31st Conference on Neural Information Processing Systems (NIPS 2017) (2017)
11. Arrieta, A.B., et al.: Explainable artificial intelligence (XAI): Concepts, taxonomies, opportunities and challenges toward responsible AI (2019). arXiv:1910.10045v2
12. Adali, T., Guido, R.C., Ho, T.K., Müller, K.R., Strather, S.: Interpretability, reproducibility and replicability Guest editoriall. IEEE Signal Process. Mag. **39**, 5–7 (2022)
13. National Academies of Sciences, Engineering and Medicine. Reproducibility and Replicability in Science. Washington DC, USA: National Academy Press (2019)
14. European Union High-level Independent Group on Artificial Intelligence. "Assessment List for Trustworthy AI" (2020). https://digital-strategy.ec.europa.eu/en/library/assessment-list-trustworthy-artificial-intelligence-altai-self-assessment.
15. Linux Foundation AI & Data's Trusted AI Committee Principles Working Group "Linux Foundation AI & Data's Principles for Trusted AI" (2021). https://lfaidata.foundation/blog/2021/02/08/lf-ai-data-announces-principles-for-trusted-ai/.
16. OECD.AI "OECD AI Principles" (2019). https://oecd.ai/en/ai-principles.
17. Nielsen, I.E., Dera, D., Rasool, G., Ramachandran, R.P., Bouaynaya, N.C.: Robust explainability. IEEE Signal Process. Mag. **39**, 73–84 (2022)
18. Bravo-Rocca, G., Liu, P., Guitart, J., Dholakia, A., Ellison, D., Hodak, M.: Human-in-the-loop online multi-agent approach to increase trustworthiness in ML models through trust scores and data augmentation. In: IEEE COMPSAC (2022)
19. Jiang, H., Kim, B., Guan, M., Gupta, M.: To trust or not to trust a classifier. In: 32nd Conference on Neural Information Processing Systems (NeurIPS 2018), Montreal, Canada (2018)
20. Devlin, J., Chang, M.W., Lee, K., Toutanova, K.: BERT: Pre-training of Deep Bidirectional Transformers for Language Understanding. arXiv preprint arXiv:1810:04805v2 (2019)
21. Radford, A., Wu, J., Child, R., Luan, D., Amodei, D., Sutskever, I.: Language models are unsupervised multitask learners (2019)
22. Rudin, C.: Stop explaining black box machine learning models for high stakes decisions and use interpretable models instead. Nat. Mach. Intell. **1**(5), 206–215 (2019)

23. Jacovi, A., Goldberg, Y.: Towards faithfully interpretable NLP systems: how should we define and evaluate faithfulness?" In: Proceedings of ACL, pp. 4198–4205 (2020)
24. Bibal, A., et al.: Is attention explanation? An introduction to the debate. In: Proceedings of the 60th Annual Meeting of the Association for Computational Linguistics, vol. 1, pp. 3889–3900 (2022)

# TPCx-AI: First Adopter's Experience Report

Hyo-Sil Kim[✉], Doohwan Kim, Byoungjun Seo, and Sejin Hwang

Telecommunications Technology Association (TTA), Seongnam, Korea
{hyosil.kim,enghks0605,sbj8388,hsejin314}@tta.or.kr

**Abstract.** This paper provides a report based on the first TPCx-AI benchmark publication.

**Keywords:** Performance · AI · TPC

## 1 TTA

### 1.1 Background of TTA

TTA, which stands for Telecommunications Technology Association, is a non-profit organization, established in 1988, created for standardization of information and communication technology (ICT) and for testing and certification of ICT products, services, and data.

Especially, TTA is funded by the Korean government to help Korean server/storage vendors advertise and extend their market share globally. To support Korean vendors, being a member of the TPC is very helpful. In particular, as a member of the TPCx-AI subcommittee, TTA could publish the first TPCx-AI result, helping that Korea servers to be in the spotlight in the global AI market.

In this paper, we share the experience of publishing the first TPCx-AI result on cluster.

### 1.2 Test Description

The test was conducted on three KTNF KR580S2 [1] server nodes. The software used included Cloudera Data Platform (CDP) version 7.1, where Hadoop 3.1 and Spark 2.4 services are provided. The operating systems used were Red Hat Enterprise Linux Server 7.8 & 7.9. All testing was conducted in conformance with the requirements of the TPCx-AI Standard Specification, Revision 1.0.1.

**Hardware configurations of the system.** The detail of the measured configuration diagram is shown in Fig. 1.

Each of the three nodes consists of two Intel® Xeon® Platinum 8380 CPUs, 2TiB memory. As a storage, one node uses 10 SSDs and the other two use 13 SSDs. Since each node works both as a Master and a Worker in CDP, each contains 1 Journal node(SSD), 1 Zookeeper node(SSD), and 6 Data nodes(SSDs) in common. One NVMe SSD is used as a Node Manager local directory to improve Spark shuffle performance for each node (for the first node, it shares with Journal node). Two SSDs are used as Name nodes for the second and the third nodes.

R. Nambiar and M. Poess (Eds.): TPCTC 2022, LNCS 13860, pp. 120–126, 2023.
https://doi.org/10.1007/978-3-031-29576-8_9

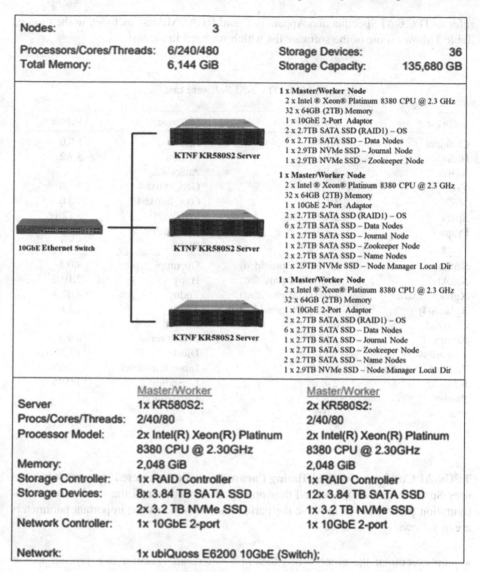

**Fig. 1.** Configuration Diagram

**Software Configurations of the System.** To run the TPCx-AI Benchmark in multi nodes, there are several prerequisite software to be installed, along with CDP 7.1: Java 8 (included in CDP), Python 3.6 or higher, Anaconda3/Conda4 or higher, GCC 9.0, Cmake 3.12 or higher, OpenMPI 4.0 or higher, and so on.

When the prerequisites are all installed, one can use setup-spark.sh script (included in the toolkit) to build TPCx-AI driver virtual environment and the driver itself. Conda allows build_dl.yml file (included in the toolkit) to be used to install prerequisite software to run the TPCx-AI use cases. For more detailed software list and toolkit setup procedure, refer to TPCx-AI Specification Appendix F and README.md included in the toolkit. Table 1 shows some of the software list which we used in the test.

**Table 1.** TPCx-AI Software List.

| Software | Version | Software | Version |
|---|---|---|---|
| Cloudera | 7.1.7 | Java | 1.8.0 |
| Hadoop | 3.1.1 | Python | 3.7.2 |
| HDFS | 3.1.1 | Anaconda | 3 |
| Yarn | 3.1.1 | Gcc_linux64 | 9.3.0 |
| MR2 | 3.1.1 | Gxx_linux64 | 9.3.0 |
| Spark | 2.4.7 | CMake | 3.12.1 |
| Pyspark | 2.4.7 | OpenMPI | 4.0.5 |
| | | Pssh | 2.3.1 |
| Scollop | 3.1.3 (TPC provided) | Openmpi_mpicc | 4.0.5 |
| Sarpkts | 0.4.1 (TPC provided) | H5py | 2.10.0 |
| Xgboost-spark | 1.0.0 (TPC provided) | Tqdm | 4.62.3 |
| Xgboost4j | 1.0.0 (TPC provided) | Joblib | 1.1.0 |
| Horovod | 0.19.1 | Librosa | 0.8.1 |
| Numpy | 1.19.2 | Petastorm | 0.9.8 |
| Tensorflow | 2.2.0 | Dlib | 19.20.0 |
| Tensorflow-addons | 0.10.0 | Libsndfile-devel | 1.0.25 |
| Keras | 2.4.3 | Libsndfile | 1.0.25 |
| Pandas | 1.3.5 | Libglvnd-glx | 1.0.1 |
| Pyarrow | 3.0.0 | | |

**TPCx-AI Configuration and Tuning Parameters.** For clustered system, TPCx-AI uses Spark to run use cases, and thus one needs to understand the spark-submit configuration parameters to improve the performance. Some of the important parameters are as follows:

- num-executors: the number of executors, where an executor is a process that is launched for a Spark application on a worker node
- executor-cores: how many CPU cores are available per executor/application
- executor-memory: memory assigned to each executor
- spark.executor.memoryOverhead: the amount of off-heap memory to be allocated per executor
- spark.sql.shuffle.partitions: configures the number of partitions to use when shuffling data for joins or aggregations.

Note that the number of CPU cores (i.e., threads) in our system is 160 for each node. We allow Spark to use 150 cores for each node, so the total number of available cores seen across three nodes is 450. Each node can use 2,048GiB memory and we allow

Spark to use 1,806GiB memory, so the total amount of available memory seen across is 5,418GiB. Considering that, we set non-deep learning use cases 1, 3, 4, 6, 7, 10 to use num-executors 89, executor-cores 5, (89 × 5 = 445 cores to be used in total), and each of them use 44 g (44 g × 89 = 3,916 g memory in total). For deep learning use cases 2, 5, 9, we set num-executors 3, executor-cores 140 (executor-cores 40 for use case 5), which results in running one executor per node. The number of Tensorflow tasks that will run in each executor is controlled by the --executor_cores_horovod and --task_cpus_horovod parameters, which will be explained later. Use case 8 is set somewhat differently from the others and we explain later. We set Spark.sql.suffle.partitions parameter such that partition size is set between 100 MB and 200 MB, where it is known to perform the best.

We summarize the Spark parameters used in the Power Training Test in Table 2. One can use parameters for Power Serving Test and Throughput Test, similarly.

**Table 2.** Spark Parameters that are used (Scale Factor = 1,000, Streams = 10).

| Parameter names | Use case 1,3,4,7 | Use case 2 | Use case 5 | Use case 6 | Use case 8 | Use case 9 | Use case 10 |
|---|---|---|---|---|---|---|---|
| num-executors | 89 | 3 | 3 | 89 | 111 | 3 | 89 |
| executor-cores | 5 | 140 | 40 | 5 | 4 | 140 | 5 |
| executor-memory | 40g | 1200g | 1200g | 40g | 40g | 1200g | 40g |
| spark.executor.memoryOverhead | 4g | 200g | 200g | 4g | 4g | 300g | 4g |
| spark.sql.shuffle.partitions | – | – | – | 2000 | 2000 | 8000 | 200 |

One important software to be installed to run deep learning use cases 2, 5, 9 is Horovod. Horovod is a distributed deep learning training framework for TensorFlow, Keras, PyTorch, and Apache MXNet [2]. It makes it easy to take a single-CPU/GPU training script and successfully scale it to train across many CPU/GPUs in parallel. Horovod plays an important role for training and serving deep learning use cases of TPCx-AI, since the performance depends on how Horovod parameters are set. The parameters that can be set in TPCx-AI is:

- task_cpus_horovod: the number of cores assigned to an Apache Spark task
- executor_cores_horovod: the number of cores assigned to an Apache Spark executor

Another important software is XGBoost4J-Spark (used to run use case 8), which integrates XGBoost and Apache Spark by fitting XGBoost to Spark's MLLIB framework [3]. The parameters of XGBoost4J-Spark take an impact on the performance, too. The parameters that can be set in TPCx-AI is:

- num-workers: controls how many parallel workers can be used when running the XGBoost Classification Model
- num-threads: the number of threads used by each XGBoost worker. Spark requires that all of num-thread multiplied by num-workers cores should be available before

the test. It is recommended that the product of num-executors and executor-cores be equal to the product of num-workers and num-threads.

- num_round: the number of boosting rounds

We summarize the use case specific parameters that can be set in TPCx-AI Power Training Phase in Table 3. By the Specification (Appendix C), only the parameters listed in the table can be changed. Note that for use case 5, task_cpus_horovod and executor_cores_horovod are set to the same values of num-executors and executor-cores, respectively, so we have no chance to change task_cpus_horovod and executor_cores_horovod differently. Power Serving Phase and Throughput Phase can be set similarly.

**Table 3.** TPCx-AI Parameters that can be set (Scale Factor = 1,000, Streams = 10).

| Use cases | Parameter names | Power Training Parameter values |
|---|---|---|
| 2 | epoch | 5 |
| | batch | 64 |
| | learning rate | 0.001 (default) |
| | task_cpus_horovod | 1 |
| | executor_cores_horovod | 4 |
| 5 | epoch | 5 |
| | batch | 4,096 |
| | learning rate | 0.001 (default) |
| 7 | num-blocks | 200 |
| 8 | num-workers | 222 |
| | num-thread | 2 |
| | num_rounds | 5 |
| 9 | epoch | 3 |
| | batch | 128 |
| | learning rate | 0.000001 (default) |
| | task_cpus_horovod | 1 |
| | executor_cores_horovd | 30 |

The last tuning parameter tip is Java Garbage Collection (GC), where we change from default Parallel GC, to G1GC to reduce the garbage collection time for JVM applications.

**TPCx-AI Result and Benchmark Running Experience.** Figure 2 shows the final result. The time to take to run each phase is shown **in** Table 4. Overall test time (Load Test, Power Training Test, Power Serving Test I, Power Serving Test II, Scoring Test, and Throughput Test) takes 57,372.169 s (about 16 h). The total data generation time is 13,406.189 s (which is not stated in FDR).

Note that the two deep learning use cases, UC 2 (the customer conversation transcription) and UC 9 (the facial recognition) dominates most of the time, and thus, tuning

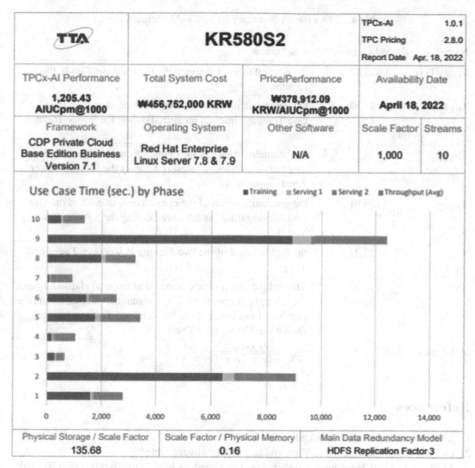

**Fig. 2.** Result Summary

their related parameters plays very important role to improve the performance. It might be seen a little bit unfair to the other use cases, especially use cases 3, 4, 7, and 10, since no matter how hard we try to reduce their time, the time for use cases 2 and 9 dominates, which is one of the drawbacks of TPCx-AI

Another drawback we think is that TPCx-AI, currently, forbid a major change of the toolkit code which makes it difficult for AI software or hardware developer to use their own libraries or models to improve the performance or accuracy.

We hope that in the future version, such drawbacks will be all redeemed.

Overall, TPCx-AI is a well-made benchmark; easy to install, easy to run, including all necessary lifecycle steps to test AI software and hardware. It was very pleased experience for us to test TPCx-AI benchmark and publish the first result. Audit process was very rigorous where it makes TPC result more credible in the IT industry. We thank Hamesh Patel, the TPCx-AI chair, and Rodrigo Escobar, the developer of the toolkit, for helping TTA to solve some of the issues came across during TPCx-AI testing and audit.

**Table 4.** TTA's Result Summary in TPCx-AI Metirc Values.

| Name | Value (seconds) | Description |
| --- | --- | --- |
| $T_{Load}/T_{LD}$ | 4,405.47 | the elapsed time of copying the input dataset files to the final location |
| $T_{PTT}$ | 981.90 | the geometric mean of the elapsed time of each of the Use case Training times as measured during the Power Training Test |
| $T_{PST1}$ | 128.21 | the geometric mean of the elapsed time of each of the Use case Serving times as measured during the Serving Power Test I |
| $T_{PST2}$ | 126.91 | the geometric mean of the elapsed time of each of the Use case Serving times as measured during the Serving Power Test II |
| $T_{PST}$ | 128.21 | the higher value of the two Serving Power tests $T_{PST1}$ and $T_{PST2}$ |
| $T_{TT}$ | 110.67 | Throughput test metric computed as the total elapsed time of the throughput test divided by the number of streams and the number of use cases in the Performance Test as measured during the Throughput Test |
| AIUCpm@SF | 1,205.43 | $\dfrac{SF*N*60}{\sqrt[4]{T_{LD}*T_{PTT}*T_{PST}*T_{TT}}}$ |

# References

1. KTNF homepage http://www.ktnf.co.kr
2. HOROVOD Homepage. https://horovod.readthedocs.io/en/stable/
3. XGBoost4J-Spark Homepage. https://xgboost.readthedocs.io/en/stable/jvm/xgboost4j_spark_tutorial.html

# New Initiatives in the TPC

Meikel Poess[✉]

Oracle Corporation, Redwood Shores, CA 94065, USA
meikel.poess@oracle.com

**Abstract.** TPC stands for *stricter standards* and *tougher tests* in system benchmarking for over 30 years, during which technology advanced enormously. In order to stay relevant the TPC had to adapt to the advancing technology or become obsolete. Initially, the business use case of computer systems was mainly focused on online transaction processing (OLTP). Hence, the TPC developed a series of OLTP benchmarks, learning valuable lessons along the way (TPC-A, TPC-B, TPC-C and TPC-E). Then the TPC ventured into other use cases such as decision support (TPC-D, TPC-H, TPC-R, TPC-DS), web applications (TPC-App), virtualization (TCP-VMS) and data integration (TPC-DI). When the TPC realized that the old way of developing benchmarks was not sustainable, it added a new way of developing benchmark, express benchmark, which resulted in a flurry of benchmark standards (TPCx-HS, TPCx-V, TPCx-BB, TPCx-HCI, TPCx-IoT and TPCx-AI). With *cloud computing* becoming more and more important, the TPC made sure that new benchmarks would be able to run in the cloud. At the same time the TPC modified its pricing specification to allow for pricing of cloud based benchmarks.

**Keywords:** Benchmark Standards · Performance Evaluation · Databases

## 1 Introduction

The Transaction Processing Performance Council (TPC[TM]), founded in 1988, can look back at a very rich history of developing industry standard benchmarks for computer systems. Without doubt these benchmarks shaped the way performance measurements have been conducted for decades.

The foundation of the TPC was mostly driven by the need to overcome a phenomenon, commonly referred to as *benchmarketing*. Using this marketing practice, organizations claim superior performance based on non-standard benchmarks. The aim of running non-standard benchmarks on a computer system is to claim superior performance by focusing on those aspects of the computer systems that are superior to those of competitors. However, these non-standard benchmarks often run workloads without well defined execution rules, no minimum requirements for component redundancy, no rules for fair pricing, no verifiable documentation of the benchmark execution including its overall correctness. This is why TPC benchmarks have been successfully used for decades and are still being used.

© The Author(s), under exclusive license to Springer Nature Switzerland AG 2023
R. Nambiar and M. Poess (Eds.): TPCTC 2022, LNCS 13860, pp. 127–148, 2023.
https://doi.org/10.1007/978-3-031-29576-8_10

Technology has rapidly advanced over the years, triggering the TPC to adapt constantly to new circumstances. Before diving into more recent developments in the TPC, I will give a brief history of past TPC benchmarks focusing on how the TPC adapted to changes in technology from the very beginning.

The TPC started by developing on-line transaction processing (OLTP) systems benchmarks. Based on the DebitCredit benchmark that Jim Gray developed in collaboration with 24 others from academia and industry [4], the TPC developed the first OLTP benchmark, TPC-A[TM] [17]. TPC-A for the first time established a level playing field by mandating production-oriented requirements, mandating the reporting of peak performance numbers that can be sustained for a reasonable amount of time, mandating ACID compliance, and a Full Disclosure Report (FDR) that discloses the complete benchmark implementation and all test output. With technology enhancing in the years following, TPC-A was replaced by TPC-B[TM] [19] and, eventually, by TPC-C[TM] [13,20]. TPC-C is still an active benchmark today, serving the benchmark community for 30 years.

## 1.1 Venturing into New Benchmark Domains

After covering the OLTP benchmark needs the TPC started developing benchmarks in other domains. Two years, after TPC-C was released, the TPC presented its first decision support (DS) benchmark, TPC-D [TM] [21]. TPC-D served the benchmark community for five years until 1999 when *Database Management Software* (DBMS) vendors invented materialized views.

The cost for creating materialized views was not adequately represented in TPC-D's performance metric causing results to sky rocket, dwarfing results of vendors without materialized view support. TPC-D was subsequently split into two separate benchmarks, the reporting decision support benchmark, TPC-R[TM] [12,23], that allowed the use of sophisticated auxiliary data structures, e.g. materialized views, and the ad-hoc decision support workload TPC-H[TM] [12,22]. While TPC-H flourished, TPC-R was retired in 2005. TPC-H is still an active benchmark with 14 results in 2021, 3 results in 2020 and 8 results in 2019.

After successfully establishing benchmarks for the OLTP and decision support domains, the TPC started developing benchmarks for emerging domains, such as *electronic commerce, virtualization, hyperconversion, big data* and *internet of things*. In parallel the TPC started working on developing updated versions for TPC-C and TPC-H.

The first benchmark in a new domain was TPC-W[TM] [12], established in 2002. It was, with minor changes, later re-branded as TPC-App[TM] [18]. It was an application server benchmark simulating the activities of a business-to-business transactional application server. While very popular in academia, TPC-App never generated many benchmark publications and was retired in 2008. For a detailed timeline of TPC benchmarks see Fig. 1.

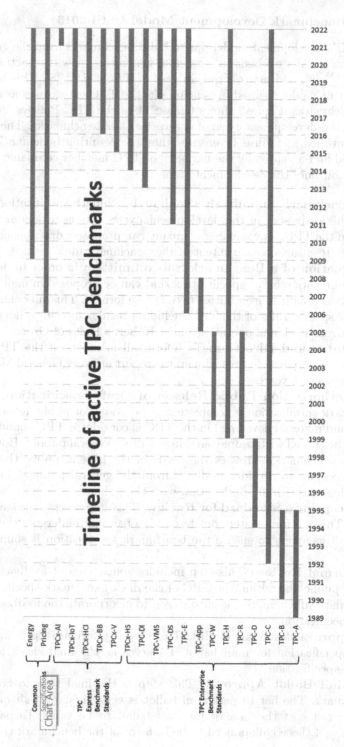

**Fig. 1.** History of TPC Benchmarks Between the Years 1989 and 2022

## 1.2  TPC's Benchmark Development Model Until 2013

Until 2013 TPC's development model was to build benchmarks from the ground up, i.e. with new database schemata, new data generators, new transactions, in case of TPC-E$^{TM}$ [6], and new queries, in case of TPC-DS$^{TM}$ [8]. This benchmark development model resulted in benchmarks the TPC categorizes as *enterprise class* benchmarks. Figure 3 shows Clause 11 of the TPC Policies Version 6.18, outlining the development cycle of enterprise class benchmarks. The eight step process outlined in Clause 11 ensures that the resulting benchmarks are technically solid and accepted by the majority of TPC member companies. The following steps outlines the development steps.

- Step 1 - **Benchmark Submittal:** The draft benchmark specification submitted in this early step in the development cycles acts as a document for discussion in the TPC. Any member company can propose a draft benchmark specification. It ensures a clear intent of the benchmark idea.
- Step 2 - **Creation of a Benchmark Subcommittee:** In order to develop the draft specification into a specification that can be proposed in mail ballot (Step 8), a benchmark subcommittee needs to be formed. This subcommittee works under specific rules of the TPC including regular meetings, documentation of current work and operating under Robert's Rules of Order.
- Step 3 - **Status and Direction:** To inform all members of the TPC the subcommittee is required to present a status report at every General Meeting (usually five times a year).
- Step 4 - **Authorization Public Release of Draft Specification:** Once the benchmark specification is complete it is proposed for public release. All discussion and material developed in the TPC is considered TPC confidential and cannot be shared with people outside the TPC (general public). However, to assure a benchmark addresses the needs of the general public the TPC deems it necessary to consider feedback from the general public. This step allows sharing of the draft specification with the public
- Step 5 - **Accepting a Standard for Review:** This step accepts the standard for review. This is a formal step, but has a high bar as it undergoes thorough review by all members to ensure the benchmark specification is sound and solid.
- Step 6 - **Formal Review:** This step includes solicitation of feedback from the general public and within the TPC of the draft benchmark specification. The benchmark subcommittee is encouraged to incorporate the feedback into the draft specification.
- Step 7 - **Approval for Mail Ballot:** This step is a formal step to approve the draft specification for mail ballot. It serves as the final check for the benchmark specification
- Step 8 - **Mail Ballot Approval:** This step is the final step to create a new benchmark. The bar to pass mail ballot is very high. $\frac{2}{3}$ of all member companies must cast their ballot for mail ballot to be valid. To pass the benchmark $\frac{2}{3}$ of those ballots need to be in favor of the benchmark (Fig. 2).

**11.2      TPC-Enterprise Benchmark Development Cycle**

The following outlines the steps for submitting a benchmark proposal and securing approval.

**11.2.1    Step 1: Benchmark Submittal**

**Member** companies will submit a draft standard specification in a format similar to **TPC Benchmark Standards**. The proposal is submitted to the **Council** and is forwarded to the **SC** for consideration. The **SC** will review the contents, applicability and potential of the proposal and present a recommendation back to the **Council**, identifying advantages/disadvantages and proposed course of action. The **Council** must then vote to formally accept the proposal for future work.

**11.2.2    Step 2: Creation of a Benchmark Subcommittee**

Given the acceptance of the proposal for future work, the **Council** will then establish and empower a **Benchmark Subcommittee** to develop a formal benchmark **Specification**. To speed-up the benchmark development cycle, the subcommittee is empowered to brief non-members on their benchmark in order to obtain timely feedback.

**11.2.3    Step 3: Status and Direction**

At each **General Meeting**, the **Benchmark Subcommittee** will provide a status update on its work, including a working draft of the **Specification**. During the **General Meeting**, the **Council** may provide direction and feedback to the subcommittee to further their work.

**11.2.4    Step 4: Authorizing Public Release of Draft Specification**

If it deems it advisable, the **Council** may authorize the release of a draft **Specification** to the public. The principal goals of releasing a draft specification are to encourage companies to implement the draft **Specification**, to gather more experimental data, and to speed up the approval of a **TPC-Enterprise Benchmark Standard**.

Within the purpose of the procedure as outlined above, companies are encouraged to run the draft **Specification**, document the results, and discuss the results with **All Members** and customers. Companies may also publish technical articles or make presentations to industry conferences in which they discuss results. However, these articles/presentations are bound by the conditions in **Policies** § 8.1 (Use of TPC Materials) and **Policies** § 8.3 (Fair Use of TPC Specifications).

**Comment**: Companies are reminded that this draft **Specification** is not a **Benchmark Standard**, and companies must adhere fully to all the provisions and restrictions of the **Fair Use Policy**. Only results published in accordance with a **Benchmark Standard** are considered **TPC Results** and can be publicized as such.

**11.2.5    Step 5: Accepting a Standard for Review**

When the **Benchmark Subcommittee** feels that the **Specification** is of sufficient quality to be considered for formal review and approval, it will submit the **Specification** to the **Council** for approval to advance into formal review. A formal review period of 60 days is customary.

**11.2.6    Step 6: Formal Review**

During this phase, the **Specification** will be made available to **All Members** and the public for formal review. All comments and proposed changes generated from the review will be **posted** to the **Private Web Site** and considered by the **Benchmark Subcommittee** for resolution.

**Comment**: **Members** and the public are reminded that this **Specification** is not a **Benchmark Standard**, and companies must adhere fully to all the provisions and restrictions of the **Fair Use Policy**. Only results published in accordance with a **Benchmark Standard** are considered **TPC Results** and can be publicized as such.

**11.2.7    Step 7: Approval for Mail Ballot**

The **Benchmark Subcommittee** will propose resolution of comments from the formal review as an updated **Specification** to **All Members** for approval by the **Council**. The **Council** approves the updated **Specification** by voting to send the **Specification** out for **Mail Ballot**.

**11.2.8    Step 8: Mail Ballot Approval**

To become a **Benchmark Standard**, the **Specification** must be approved by a **Mail Ballot** in accordance with **Policies** § 4.5 and **Policies** § 11.3.1.

In the event the **Mail Ballot** is not approved, the benchmark development work will automatically cease. If the benchmark development was the only work of the **Benchmark Subcommittee**, the subcommittee will be disbanded at the conclusion of the next **General Meeting** if the **Council** does not authorize continued work.

**Fig. 2.** Clause 11 of the TPC Policies Version 6.18: Enterprise Class Benchmark Development Cycle

The TPC realized that the existing approach to developing Enterprise Class benchmarks, e.g. TPC-C, TPC-D and TPC-App, took too much resources in the TPC and their member companies, causing long benchmark development cycles and, thus, late time to market. The main reasons for the long development time was (i) following the stiff development model with its many approval steps involving super majority of the entire TPC membership, (ii) building of benchmarks from the ground-up and (iii) defining technology agnostic benchmarks

The existing development model, which requires many level of approval, gave a lot of opportunity to lobby for or against benchmarks. Especially, the final mail ballot approval step marked a high bar for establishing a new benchmark. For the following example I assume a total TPC membership of 22 companies. In order for a mail ballot to be valid, $\frac{2}{3}$ of all member companies must cast their ballot, e.g. $\lceil \frac{2}{3} * 22 \rceil = 15$. Usually voter participation is less than 100%. Let's assume there is a 91% voter participation, that is, 2 member companies do not plan to cast their votes regardless. If a small group of active member companies, e.g. 4 (Group Of Four), do not wanted an enterprise class benchmark to pass, Group Of Four would only need to convince another 2 active member companies not to cast their ballots for the entire mail ballot to be invalid. Assuming the Group Of Four fails to convince 2 active member companies not to cast their ballot, and, as a result, 20 member companies cast their votes, then mail ballot is valid. However, for the benchmark to pass it requires $\lceil \frac{2}{3} * 20 \rceil = 14$ *yes* votes. At that time, the Group Of Four would only need to convince 2 more companies to vote *abstain*.

Apart from the bureaucratic and political hurdles outlined in the above paragraph, developing an enterprice class benchmark is also very resource intensive. One of the main reasons is the amount of data needed to populate a meaningful database for performance testing purposes. Data generation must be reliable, fast and realistic. Early TPC benchmarks developed their own data generators, such as TPC-C, TPC-E, TPC-H and TPC-DS. However, due to the time it took to develop these generators, the TPC started utilizing data generator frameworks, such as the parallel data generation framework PDGF [14]. PDGF greatly reduced the time to develop a reliable and fast data generator.

Enterprise class benchmarks are technology agnostic. They do not mandate the use of any specific technology/technique to execute the workload specified in the benchmark specification. For instance, TPC-H does not specify any particular Data Definition Language (DDL) for the creation of its eight tables, including data types. Instead, TPC-H defines the minimum requirement for data types.

Figure 3 shows Clause 1.3 of the TPC-H specification. It defines pseudo data types, e.g. *identifier*, and their requirements. A column using the datatype *identifier* must be able to hold any key value generated for the column by the data generator and be able to support at least 2,147,483,647 unique values. A benchmark implementation of TPC-H can use any of the database datatypes as long as the datatype supports the above requirements. However, the implementation datatype chosen by the implementation for a particular datatype definition

## 1.3 Datatype Definitions

1.3.1 The following datatype definitions apply to the list of columns of each table:

- **Identifier** means that the column must be able to hold any key value generated for that column and be able to support at least 2,147,483,647 unique values;

**Comment**: A common implementation of this datatype will be an integer. However, for SF greater than 300 some column values will exceed the range of integer values supported by a 4-byte integer. A test sponsor may use some other datatype such as 8-byte integer, decimal or character string to implement the identifier datatype;

- **Integer** means that the column must be able to exactly represent integer values (i.e., values in increments of 1) in the range of at least -2,147,483,646 to 2,147,483,647.
- **Decimal** means that the column must be able to represent values in the range -9,999,999,999.99 to +9,999,999,999.99 in increments of 0.01; the values can be either represented exactly or interpreted to be in this range;
- **Big Decimal** is of the Decimal datatype as defined above, with the additional property that it must be large enough to represent the aggregated values stored in temporary tables created within query variants;
- **Fixed text, size N** means that the column must be able to hold any string of characters of a fixed length of N.

**Comment:** If the string it holds is shorter than N characters, then trailing spaces must be stored in the database or the database must automatically pad with spaces upon retrieval such that a CHAR_LENGTH() function will return N.

- **Variable text, size N** means that the column must be able to hold any string of characters of a variable length with a maximum length of N. Columns defined as "variable text, size N" may optionally be implemented as "fixed text, size N";
- **Date** is a value whose external representation can be expressed as YYYY-MM-DD, where all characters are numeric. A date must be able to express any day within at least 14 consecutive years. There is no requirement specific to the internal representation of a date.

**Comment:** The implementation datatype chosen by the test sponsor for a particular datatype definition must be applied consistently to all the instances of that datatype definition in the schema, except for identifier columns, whose datatype may be selected to satisfy database scaling requirements.

1.3.2 The symbol SF is used in this document to represent the scale factor for the database (see Clause 4: ).

**Fig. 3.** Clause 1.5 of TPC-H: Data type Definitions

must be applied consistently to all occurrences of that datatype definition in the schema (see comment in Clause 1.3.1).

There are many advantages, but also crucial disadvantages to this benchmark class. One important advantage of enterprise class benchmarks is that they allow the use of technology that was not anticipated at the time the benchmarks was designed. As a consequence, enterprise class benchmarks encourage the development of technology that may lead to better performance results. On the other hand technology agnostic benchmarks make it much more difficult to define sound benchmark rules that do not open the door for technology that break the benchmark/make it obsolete, as happened to TPC-D.

## 1.3 Express Benchmarks™, a Benchmark Model for Rapid Benchmark Development

To reduce benchmark development time and approval time for incremental improvements of benchmarks, the TPC established a new benchmark class, named express benchmarks[TM] [7] in 2013. Express class benchmarks are following the same rigorous development rules as enterprise class benchmarks. However, instead of requiring a separate benchmark implementation by the test sponsor, they allow a test sponsor to download a benchmark suite, a.k.a. *kit*, that runs the entire benchmark.

A kit based benchmark is self contained and limited to the hardware and software it is designed for. This reduces the benchmark development time as no comprehensive wording to define the benchmark needs to be developed, nor does the code need to be developed for all possible hardware and software combinations. It also opens the door for the development of a TPC benchmark based on open source software.

The bar to run an express class benchmark is much lower compared to that of an enterprise class benchmark. Benchmark sponsors[1] do not have to implement an express class benchmark as the kit provides the necessary implementation. The audit process of an express class benchmark is also much easier. Instead of undergoing an audit with a TPC certified auditor including the scheduling of the audit, waiting for the results from the auditor, paying the auditor, certification of express class benchmarks results can be done by TPC peers in a *pre-publication board* (PPB). It is, however, possible to have an audit of an express class benchmark be certified by a TPC certified auditor.

## 2    TPC Express Benchmarks[TM] Becoming Reality

The introduction of the express benchmark class resulted in an enormous increase in new benchmark development. The last Enterprise Class benchmark, TPC-DI[TM] [11,20], hit the market in 2013 after $5\frac{1}{2}$ years of development, from April 2008 to October 2013.

After that a new era of express class benchmark development began. The first express class benchmark was TPCx-HS[TM] [1,2,9], a *big data system benchmark*. TPCx-HS, published in 2014, marked a major turning point in benchmark development in the TPC, as it's development is based on the existing open source benchmark, TeraSort. Ironically, Terasort itself was based on a benchmark originally proposed by Jim Gray, *Sort Scan* [4]. Two years later TPCx-BB[TM] [24] [5] was published, TPC's first *end-to-end big data benchmark*. It is largely based on TPC-DS. In 2017 three Express Benchmarks[TM] followed, TPCx-V[TM] [15,27], TPCx-HCI[TM] [16,25] and TPCx-IoT[TM] [10,26]. TPCx-V and TPCx-HCI are virtualization benchmarks. TPCx-V is based on TPC-E and TPCx-HCI is based on TPC-V. TPCx-IoT is the first end-to-end benchmark for measuring *internet of things* systems.

## 3    Big Data Benchmarks

*Big data* is a term coined to describe processing of very large data datasets. These datasets have three properties: Volume, Velocity, and Variety. Volume reflects the

---

[1] A benchmark sponsor is a company or multiple companies that run a TPC benchmark and publish its result on the TPC website.

size of the dataset, which is usually measured in Terabytes. Velocity stands for the speed at which data is generated. Variety represents the structure in which data is generated. In traditional database management systems data gathered in real life is transformed into a coherent structured form, i.e. tables, a.k.a. entities. However, recent years have shown that a large percent of data captured in real life cannot be easily transformed into a structured form. These kind of data is considered semi-structured and un-structured. An example for semi-structured data are user clicks from a retailer's website, which are extracted from a web server log. They can vary in format due to their action type. An example of un-structured data is information from product reviews that are commonly used for sentiment analysis. These are usually provided by customers in free form text.

**TPCx-HS** marks TPC's first big data benchmark and its first express class Benchmark. Based on the TeraSort benchmark, TPCx-HS is considered a system level benchmark measuring hardware, operating system and commercial Apache HDFS API compatible software distributions. It adapted TeraSort's data model, including its data generator, and added TPC's stringent formal benchmark rules for implementation, execution, metric calculation, result verification, result publication and system pricing. TPCx-HS models a continuous system availability of 24 by 7. TPCx-HS defines the usual three primary metrics of any TPC benchmark, *performance metric*, *price-performance* and *system availability*. The performance metric is HSph@SF, the effective sort throughput of the benchmarked configuration:

$$HSph@SF = \frac{SF * 3600}{T}$$

where:

- $SF \in \{1, 3, 10, 30, 100, 300, 1000, 3000, 10000\}$ is the scale factor, indicating the amount of data to be sorted in terabyte, and
- T is the total elapsed time for the run in seconds.

TPCx-HS price-performance metric is defined as:

$$\$/HSph@SF = \frac{P}{HSph@SF}$$

where:

- P is the total cost of ownership of the *system under test* (SUT[2]). P includes the hardware and software components present in the SUT, a communication interface that can support user interface devices, additional operational components configured on the test system, and maintenance on all of the above for a three year period, and

---

[2] The system under test is essentiall the benchmark configuration, i.e. all hardware components used to run the benchmark and price the particular benchmark run. SUT is a TPC term that is used in all benchmarks.

– HSph@SF is the system performance as defined above.

TPCx-HS' System Availability Date is defined in the TPC pricing specification [3] as the time the SUT is available for general purchase.

In addition to the above main metrics, TPCx-HS also reports the following numerical quantities:

– $T_G$: Data generation phase completion time with HSGen reported in hh:mm:ss format,
– $T_s$: Data sort phase completion time with HSSort reported in hh:mm:ss format, and
– $T_V$: Data validation phase completion time reported in hh:mm:ss format.

The Hadoop ecosystem is moving fast beyond batch processing with MapReduce. In 2016 the TPC introduced TPCx-HS Version 2. Based on TPCx-HS Version 1, Version 2 added support for Apache Spark - a popular platform for in-memory data processing that enables real-time analytics on Apache Hadoop. In addition, TPCx-HS Version 2 supports MapReduce (MR2). Publications on traditional on-premise and clouds deployments. Benchmark publications from TPCx-HS Version 1 and Version 2 are not comparable.

**TPCx-BB** is an end-to-end benchmark designed to measure the performance of the software and hardware components of data processing systems when executing big data tasks. These tasks uncover hidden data patterns, unknown data correlations, market trends, customer preferences and other useful information that can help organizations make informed business decisions. TPCx-BB models the big data aspect of a large retail company with physical and online presence. The workload is comprised of 30 use-cases, each representing a realistic big data problem in the form of queries and machine learning tasks that execute on large scale datasets, ranging from one terabyte to multiple Petabytes.

Big data problems are especially complex when big data frameworks, such as Apache Hadoop, are used to extract meaningful information from large datasets. Such complexity results mainly from enabling parallel data processing in a distributed fashion across multiple nodes. Currently the TPCx-BB workloads are implemented to be executed on Hadoop-based and Alibaba's MaxCompute platforms. It can be easily extended to other platforms.

TPCx-BB, like any other TPC benchmark, defines three primary metrics, the performance metric BBQpm@SF, reflecting the TPCx-BB Queries per minute throughput, the price/performance metric $/BBQpm@SF and the system availability date.

The performance metric is defined as:

$$BBQpm@SF = \frac{SF * 60 * M}{T_{LD} + \sqrt{T_{PT} * T_{TT}}} \qquad (1)$$

The enumerator is adjusted by the data set size, i.e. scale factor (SF) to allow for larger configuration having a larger overall metric. This is solely done

to encourage benchmarking larger scale factors. Without this adjustment configurations running larger scale factors might achieve lower or equal performances
than systems running smaller scale factors, although their performance is equal.
I will demonstrate this with a simple example. Let's assume a system A, running
at scale factor 1 achieves $BBQpm@SF = 100$. Let's further assume a system B
with 100 times more power (compute and IO) runs at scale factor 100. Assuming
perfect scalability of the workload from SF=1 to SF=100 and from system A to
system B, system A would finish the 100 times larger workload in the same time
system A finished its workload. With no scale factor adjustment they would both
report the same $BBQpm@SF = 100$. To showcase that system B's workload is
100 times larger than that of system A, the metric is adjusted by mulitplying
the result by the scale factor.

The denominator is the sum of the adjusted elapsed time of the load test and
the geometric mean of the adjusted elapsed times of the power and throughput
tests. The elapsed time of the *Load Test* measured in seconds is

$$T_{Load} \tag{2}$$

In real life system are reloaded rarely. Thereby, the TPC decided that only
10% of the elapsed time of the load, $T_{Load}$, should contribute to the load metric.
Hence, the elapsed time of the Load Test $T_{Load}$ is multiplied by the Multiplication
Factor (MF).

$$T_{LD} = MF * T_{Load} \tag{3}$$

The number of queries in TPCx-BB is

$$M = 30 \tag{4}$$

The geometric mean of the elapsed time $Q(i)$ $(1 \leq i \leq M)$ in seconds of each
of the $M$ queries as measured during the Power Test, multiplied by the number
of queries in the benchmark is:

$$T_{PT} = M * \sqrt[M]{\prod_{i=1}^{i=M} Q(i)} \tag{5}$$

The throughput test metric, $T_{TT}$, is computed as the total elapsed time of
the throughput test $T_{Tput}$ divided by the number of streams, $n$.

$$T_{TT} = \frac{1}{n} * T_{Tput} \tag{6}$$

## 3.1   Virtualization Benchmarks, TPCx-V and TPCx-HCI

**TPCx-V** is a Virtualization Benchmark for Database Workloads. It measures
the performance of a virtualized server platform under a demanding database
workload. It stresses CPU and memory hardware, storage, networking, hyper-
visor, and the guest operating system. TPCx-V workload is database-centric

and models many properties of cloud services, such as multiple VMs running at different load demand levels, and large fluctuations in the load level of each VM. The execution rules of the benchmark include performing a database load, running the workload, validating the results, and even performing many of the routine audit steps. Another unique characteristic of TPCx-V is an elastic workload that varies the load delivered to each of the VMs by as much as 16x, while maintaining a constant load at the host level.

The Performance Metric reported by TPCx-V measures the number of completed Trade-Result transactions expressed in transactions-per second-V (tpsV). Multiple Transactions are used to simulate the business activity of processing a trade, and each Transaction is subject to a Response Time constraint.

**TPCx-HCI** is a benchmark for *Hyper-Converged Infrastructure* (HCI). It measures the performance of Hyper-Converged Infrastructure under a demanding database workload. It stresses the virtualized hardware and software of converged storage, networking, and compute resources of the measured HCI platform. The short development time of TPCx-HCI can be attributed to the fact that it leverages many elements of TPCx-V. Results of the two benchmarks are, however, not comparable. The number of virtual machines (VM) is calculated differently for the two benchmarks. The TPCx-HCI workload is database-centric and models many properties of cloud services, such as multiple VMs running at different load demand levels, and large fluctuations in the load level of each VM. The TPCx-HCI benchmarking kit, which was developed from scratch, is a complete end-to-end kit that loads the databases, runs the benchmark, validates the results, and even performs many of the routine audit steps. Two of the main unique characteristics of TPCx-HCI are:

- It has an elastic workload that varies the load delivered to each of the VMs by as much as 16x, while maintaining a constant load at the cluster level. Sustaining optimal throughput for this elastic workload on a multi-node HCI cluster would typically benefit from frequent migrations of VMs to rebalance the load across nodes. This property measures the efficiency of VM migration as well as the uniformity of access to data from all the nodes.
- In the Data Accessibility test of TPCx-HCI, a node is powered down ungracefully, and the benchmark continues to run on the other nodes. The test sponsor has to include a throughput graph for this test, demonstrating the impact on performance, as well as report the recovery time to regain resilience.

## 3.2   TPCx-IoT

The *internet of things* (IoT) is a term that describes groups of physical devices, a.k.a. "things", that communicate to each other over the *internet*. These devices (sensors) collect data and/or act on data (actuators). The complexity of IoT devices ranges from ordinary household objects, e.g., switches, plugs and home appliances, to sophisticated industrial applications, such as those used in agricultural, manufacturing and energy sectors, e.g.: smart fertilizer systems and digital control systems. The number of IoT devices currently deployed is estimated to be in the tens of billions. A typical IoT system is designed in a three-tier architecture:

- *Edge Tier*: sensors/actuators send data usually at very high frequencies (usually analog signals) to edge devices. Edge devices convert the analog signals into digital signals and send that data to the gateway systems.
- *Gateway Tier*: gateway database management systems serve as a short-term persistent storage. In many cases they also perform lightweight local analytics by filtering and aggregating data (dashboard-like functionality).
- *Datacenter Tier*: back-end database systems receive data from potentially multiple gateways at low frequencies and store that data long-term to perform complex global analytics.

TPCx-IoT is the first IoT benchmark specifically designed to measure the performance of *IoT gateway systems*. It enables direct comparison of different software and hardware solutions. Using the operational model of a typical electric utility provider with thousands of power substations, TPCx-IoT provides verifiable performance, price-performance and availability metrics for commercially available systems that typically ingest massive amounts of data from large numbers of devices, while running real-time analytic queries. Its flexible design allows TPCx-IoT to be used to assess a broad range of system topologies and implementation methodologies in a technically rigorous and directly comparable manner. TPCx-IoT defines three primary metrics: *performance metric, price-performance* and *system availability*. The performance metric, *IoTps*, represents the effective throughput capability of the gateway, where $SF$ is the Scale Factor (amount of data ingested) and $T$ is the ingestion elapsed time in seconds.

$$IoTps = \frac{SF}{T} \tag{7}$$

The Price-Performance metric represents the total cost of ownership of the system over three years for each thousand Transactions. $P$ is the total cost of ownership of the SUT. The first version of TPCx-IoT reported price-performance for each transaction. The reason for reporting the price-performance for each thousand transactions in Version 2 of TPCx-IoT is, because of system prices reducing and performance of systems increasing resulted in very small price-performance numbers with significant digits in the 3rd position after the decimal.

$$\$kIoTps = \frac{1000 * P}{IoTps} \tag{8}$$

### 3.3 Enterprise and Express Class Publications

Figure 4 shows the number of benchmark publications in both the Enterprise Class and the Express Class categories (Table 1).

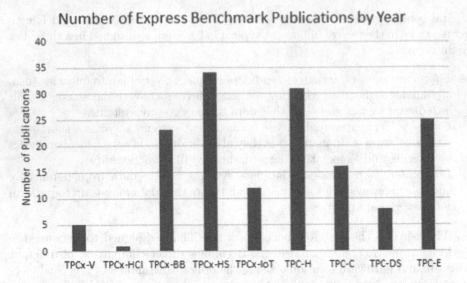

**Fig. 4.** Enterprise and Express Class Benchmark Publications since 2014

**Table 1.** Comparison Enterprise Class and Express Class Benchmark Specifications.

|  | Enterprise Class | Express Class |
|---|---|---|
| Specification Type | Written Specification with some TPC provided code | Complete KIT that runs the benchmark end-to-end |
| Tuning | Best possible optimization allowed due to custom implementation | Limited tuning based on what is allowed in KIT |
| Audit | Audit by TPC certified auditor | Peer audit, organized by member companies in Pre Publication Board (PPB) |
| Member Publication Cost | $1,250 | $500 |
| Non-Member Publication Cost | $2,500 | $750 |
| Approval Major Revision | $\frac{2}{3}$ of member companies in Council Meeting | $\frac{2}{3}$ of member companies in mail ballot |

## 4  TPC Derived Benchmarks

In recent years the TPC noticed a new trend in the benchmark community: Publication of system performance numbers using benchmarks based on TPC benchmarks. This trend resonates to the situation in the early 80s during which companies engaged in benchmarketing. In the 80s companies modified versions of their competitor's benchmarks, while today companies use, for the most part, benchmarks derived from original TPC benchmarks. In many cases they modify a TPC benchmark by simplifying the execution rules and workload (transactions/queries). For instance, benchmarks derived from TPC-DS might only perform a Database Load Test and a Power Run Test with a subset of TPC-DS' original 99 queries.

## 4.1 Initiative to Allow the Use of TPC Benchmark Material in Non-TPC Benchmarks

Instead of battling companies that use benchmarks derived from TPC benchmarks, the TPC started an initiative to allow the use of TPC benchmark material in Non-TPC benchmarks under very specific rules. This initiative amended the TPC policies. The amendments to the TPC policies include a definition of Non-TPC Benchmark Standard, rules on how TPC benchmark names and metrics may be used and a specific disclaimer to easily identify Non-TPC Benchmark Standards.

Figure 5 shows Clause 0.2.36 of the TPC policies that defines Non-TPC Benchmark Standards.

---

**0.2.36**  **Non-TPC Benchmark Standard**. A derived implementation of a **TPC Benchmark Standard** that does not maintain all the requirements of the **TPC Benchmark Standard** from which it is derived.

**Fig. 5.** Definition of a Non-TPC Benchmark Standard

---

In order to protect TPC's benchmarks from misuse and to clearly differentiate results from Non-TPC Benchmark Standards from results obtained with TPC Benchmark Standards, the TPC mandates that all public material describing work that is derived from TPC material to prefix all instances of Non-TPC Benchmark Standard with "Derived from". Furthermore, if a Non-TPC Benchmark Standard is too similar to the TPC Benchmark Standard, it will be subject to the TPC Fair Use rules (see Fig. 6).

---

**8.1.4**  **Use of the TPC Benchmark Name and Metrics**

If a party wishes to use the **TPC Benchmark Standard** name in public material to describe work that is derived from **TPC** material, the prefix "Derived from" must appear before all instances of the **TPC Benchmark Standard** name, e.g. "Derived from TPC-DS Query 82". The derived work must be a subset or clearly be different from the **TPC Benchmark Standard**. If the derived work is judged to be too similar to the **TPC Benchmark Standard**, it will be subject to the **TPC** Fair Use rules (**Policies** § 8.2)  For this reason, parties wishing to use the **TPC Benchmark Standard** name in relation to derived work must secure the **TPC**'s written permission.

The use of any **Primary Metric** or **Optional Metric** of a **TPC Benchmark Standard** in a work that is derived from **TPC** material is not allowed.

**Fig. 6.** Use of the TPC Benchmark Name and Metrics

Furthermore, all work derived from TPC Benchmarks must include a specific disclaimer. Figure 7 shows the exact wording in Clause 8.1.4 of the TPC policies that defines this disclaimer.

**8.1.5     TPC Benchmark Disclaimer**

All work derived from **TPC Benchmark Standard**s must have the following disclaimer:

This workload is derived from the **<TPC Benchmark Standard** name> Benchmark and is not comparable to published **<TPC Benchmark Standard** name> Benchmark results, as this implementation does not comply with the **<TPC Benchmark Standard** name> Benchmark.

For example, "This workload is derived from the TPC-E Benchmark and is not comparable to published TPC-E Benchmark results, as this implementation does not comply with all requirements of the TPC-E Benchmark".

**Fig. 7.** TPC Benchmark Disclaimer

## 4.2    TPC's Open Source Initiative

Another initiative, the TPC started to foster the use of Non-TPC Benchmark Standards in a regulated way, is the TPC-OSS$^{TM}$ initiative. It embraces benchmark community driven development and testing, brings the TPC closer to the new generation of benchmark developers that expect access to source code and makes the TPC brand known in the developer community. The TPC-OSS collaborated with HammerDB starting in May 2019. HammerDB is well known in the open source community and has been one of the first open source products to use TPC based benchmarks. To bring the TPC and HammerDB communities together the HammerDB source code was moved to the TPC-Council GitHub repository.

HammerDB is a benchmark Tool Kit that runs benchmarks derived from TPC benchmarks against the following DBMS: Oracle, SQL Server, Db2, Times Ten, MySQL, MariaDB, PostgreSQL, Greenplum, Postgres Plus Advanced Server, Amazon Aurora and Redshift. HammerDB currently implements an OLTP workload based derived from TPC-C, named TPROC-C and an analytical workload derived from TPC-H, named TPROC-H. For each of these TPC derived benchmarks HammerDB creates a database schema, loads the schema with data from TPC provided code and executes the workload. Unlike the original TPC benchmarks, TPC-C and TPC-H, HammerDB provides an end-to-end KIT to execute the workload, making it very easy for anybody to run these complicated workloads.

The first version of HammerDB to be hosted in the TPC GitHub repository was Version 3.3 in November 2019. Since then, the TPC has released 7 follow up releases listed in Table 2.

**Table 2.** HammerDB Release in the TPC GitHub Repository

| Release | Release Date |
|---------|--------------|
| 3.3 | 11-14-2019 |
| 4.0 | 11-26-2020 |
| 4.1 | 4-2-2021 |
| 4.2 | 7-9-2021 |
| 4.3 | 11-19-21 |
| 4.4 | 3-3-22 |
| 4.5 | 7-22-22 |
| 4.6 | 12-1-22 |

# 5   TPCx-AI™, First End-To-End AI benchmark Standard

TPCx-AI, released Sept 7, 2021 is the first end-to-end benchmark standard for measuring the performance of machine learning and data science platform. The benchmark emulates the behavior of representative industry AI solutions that are relevant in current production data centers and cloud environments. TPCx-AI is an express benchmark and, therefore, it can be easily set up in minutes by downloading the benchmark kit that is provided by the TPC (Fig. 8).

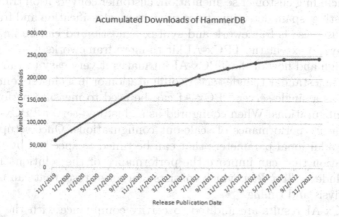

**Fig. 8.** Accumulated Downloads HammerDB

TPCx-AI addresses the needs of technology providers of both hardware and software companies, companies adopting AI in production environments, companies comparing performance and price performance (TCO), academia researching new AI approaches for large representative data sets (Text, audio, image).

TPX-AI's data generator is an extension of the *Parallel Data Generation Framework* (PDGF). PDGF is a parallel data generator that can produce large amounts of data for arbitrary schemas. The version of PDGF included in the TPCx-AI kit generates the entire TPCx-AI Test data set. PDGF's internal mechanism allow for fast generation of large data because it leverages all CPUs of a systems by running in parallel.

PDGF generates a diverse and representative data set starting at 1GB data set size up to 10TB data set size. It does that by scaling a base data set to larger data sets that resemble the same characteristic as the base data set. The base data set was assembled from different sources and contains different formats.

The data management stages, and data science pipeline modeled by the benchmark address complex business problems with the intent to answer specific business questions. The data management stages like cleansing, exploration and preprocessing mimic modern commercial pipelines that are used in current production environments Specifically, the data management stages employ training, serving and scoring phases.

Because of TPCx-AI being an end-to-end benchmark running a realistic workload on realistic data, the measured price-performance metric and the maintenance requirements for each result can be used to compare the viability of the commercially available solutions.

TPCx-AI includes 10 use cases. Each use cases defines a single problem solved by the *Deep Learning* and *Machine Learning Data Science Pipeline*. Almost all use cases included in TPCx-AI include data generation, data management, training, scoring and serving phases. The use cases describe real customer problems including customer segmentation, customer conversation transcription, sales forecasting, spam detection, price prediction, classification and fraud detection. Each use case is framework and syntax agnostic and can be implemented in many ways to extent the TPCx-AI kit to more frameworks.

The design and flow of the TPCx-AI kit makes it very easy to run the entire benchmark in a standard single-server configuration or in a cluster configuration. Configured as a single-server TPCx-AI can be used to measure performance of scale-up configurations. When configured as a clustered-server TPCx-AI can be used to measure performance of scale-out configurations. Once setup, the user can specify additional parameters that can be tuned as specified by the TPCx-AI specification that can improve the performance of the solution. TPCx-AI's kit also includes a *Test Run*, which consists of a set of tests that can be used for system analysis and tuning.

All TPCx-AI results are audited to certify compliance with the spirit and letter of the TPCx-AI Benchmark Standard by a TPC Certified auditor or a PPB.

Each benchmark run of the kit starts with a *Load Test*, followed by a *Power Training Test*, two *Power Serving tests*, a *Srocing test* and a *Throughput Test*. The Load Test is the process of copying the input data set files to the final location from where they will be accessed to execute each one of the subsequent benchmark phases. The Power Training Test measures the speed that the SUT processes the training phase of all 10 use cases. The result of the training test are the training model files for each of the use cases. The Power Serving tests measure the speed that the SUT process the serving stages of all 10 use cases. The Scoring Test, a separate serving phase, is executed in sequence for all 10 use cases against a newly generated data (excluding the truth labels) and the resulting labels from separate serving phase are compared with the ground truth labels to determine the accuracy metric or whether an error incurred by any use case. The Throughput Tests measure the ability of the system to process the most serving use cases in the least amount of time with multiple users.

TPCx-AI, as all TPC benchmarks, defines three primary metrics, the performance metric, AIUCpm@SF, the price-performance metric, $/AIUCpm@SF, and the system availability date. Furthermore, TPCx-AI defines the following secondary metrics. The *Computed Load Metric* $T_{LD}$ is the elapsed time of the Load Test in seconds.

$$T_{LD} = T_{Load} \tag{9}$$

The *Computed Power Training Test Metric* $T_{PTT}$ is the geometric mean of the elapsed times UT of each of the use case training times. $UT(i)$ is the elapsed time in seconds of the use case $i$ during the Power Training Test and $N$ is the number of use cases in the benchmark.

$$T_{PTT} = \sqrt[N]{\prod_{i=1}^{i=N} UT(i)} \tag{10}$$

The *Computed Power Serving Test Metric* $TPST$ is the maximum of two power run metrics $T_{PST1}$ and $T_{PST2}$.

$T_{PSTn}$ is the geometric mean of the elapsed time US in seconds of each of the Use Case Serving times as measured during the Serving Power Test $n \in 1, 2$.

$$T_{PSTn} = \sqrt[N]{\prod_{i=1}^{i=N} UTn(i)} \tag{11}$$

$$T_{PST} = max(T_{PST1}, T_{PST2}) \tag{12}$$

$T_{TT}$ is the throughput test metric computed as the total elapsed time of the throughput test $T_{TPUT}$ divided by the number of streams, $S$ and the number of use case in the Performance Test, $N$ as measured during the throughput test.

$$T_{TT} = \frac{T_{TPUT}}{N * S} \tag{13}$$

Using Eqs. 9 to 13 the primary performance metric is defined as:

$$AIUCpm@SF = \frac{SF * N * 60}{\sqrt[4]{T_{LD} * T_{PTT} * T_{PST} * T_{TT}}} \tag{14}$$

## 5.1  Allowing Cloud Based Benchmark Publications

When cloud computing became mainstream, it seemed straight forward to say that TPC benchmarks are ready to run in the cloud. However, like in many other situations, the devil is in the detail. One of the largest differences between publishing benchmarks in the cloud compared to on-prem is pricing.

Prior to 2005 each TPC benchmark defined its own pricing rules. In 2005 the TPC released the pricing specification, which consolidated most of the pricing wording into a separate document that each benchmark referred to. The pricing specification ended up defining a new benchmark category, named *common benchmarks*. Another benchmark in this category is the TPC-Energy specification, released in 2012. With the second major release of the pricing specification in November 2014, the TPC introduced wording to support the pricing of TPC benchmarks ran in cloud environments.

## 6  Conclusion

In this paper I gave an overview of how the TPC has been re-inventing itself over the course of 30 years. Starting with benchmarks for only one business use case (OLTP), the TPC developed benchmarks for other business uses cases, i.e. DSS, web commerce, virtualization, internet of things and artificial intelligence, as computer systems were deployed in those business use cases. The TPC also introduced new benchmarks specifications for aging benchmark specifications, such as TPC-E for TPC-C, TPC-DS for TPC-H. The TPC is constantly looking at how it can better develop benchmarks, which led to the introduction of express class benchmarks and the open source initiative, that is trying to make the TPC more attractive for new developers being used to the open source approach to software and benchmark development. Lastly we have shown how the TPC reacted to new compute environments, such as the cloud.

## References

1. https://www.tpc.org/tpcx-hs/default5.asp
2. https://www.tpc.org/TPC_Documents_Current_Versions/pdf/TPCX-HS_v2.0.3. pdf
3. https://www.tpc.org/TPC_Documents_Current_Versions/pdf/TPC-Energy_v1.5. 0.pdf
4. Bitton, D., et al.: A measure of transaction processing power. Datamation **31**(7), 112–118 (1985)
5. Ghazal, A., et al.: BigBench: towards an industry standard benchmark for big data analytics. In: Ross, K.A., Srivastava, D., Papadias, D. (eds.) Proceedings of the ACM SIGMOD International Conference on Management of Data, SIGMOD 2013, New York, NY, USA, 22–27 June 2013, pp. 1197–1208. ACM (2013). https://doi. org/10.1145/2463676.2463712
6. Hogan, T.: Overview of TPC benchmark E: the next generation of OLTP benchmarks. In: Nambiar, R., Poess, M. (eds.) TPCTC 2009. LNCS, vol. 5895, pp. 84–98. Springer, Heidelberg (2009). https://doi.org/10.1007/978-3-642-10424-4_7

7. Huppler, K., Johnson, D.: TPC express – a new path for TPC benchmarks. In: Nambiar, R., Poess, M. (eds.) TPCTC 2013. LNCS, vol. 8391, pp. 48–60. Springer, Cham (2014). https://doi.org/10.1007/978-3-319-04936-6_4

8. Nambiar, R.O., Poess, M.: The making of TPC-DS. In: Dayal, U., et al. (eds.) Proceedings of the 32nd International Conference on Very Large Data Bases, Seoul, Korea, 12–15 September 2006, pp. 1049–1058. ACM (2006). http://dl.acm.org/citation.cfm?id=1164217

9. Nambiar, R., et al.: Introducing TPCx-HS: the first industry standard for benchmarking big data systems. In: Nambiar, R., Poess, M. (eds.) TPCTC 2014. LNCS, vol. 8904, pp. 1–12. Springer, Cham (2015). https://doi.org/10.1007/978-3-319-15350-6_1

10. Poess, M., Nambiar, R., Kulkarni, K., Narasimhadevara, C., Rabl, T., Jacobsen, H.: Analysis of TPCx-IoT: the first industry standard benchmark for IoT gateway systems. In: 34th IEEE International Conference on Data Engineering, ICDE 2018, Paris, France, 16–19 April 2018, pp. 1519–1530. IEEE Computer Society (2018). https://doi.org/10.1109/ICDE.2018.00170

11. Poess, M., Rabl, T., Jacobsen, H., Caufield, B.: TPC-DI: the first industry benchmark for data integration. Proc. VLDB Endow. 7(13), 1367–1378 (2014). https://doi.org/10.14778/2733004.2733009. http://www.vldb.org/pvldb/vol7/p1367-poess.pdf

12. Pöss, M., Floyd, C.: New TPC benchmarks for decision support and web commerce. SIGMOD Rec. 29(4), 64–71 (2000). https://doi.org/10.1145/369275.369291

13. Raab, F.: TPC-C - the standard benchmark for online transaction processing (OLTP). In: Gray, J. (ed.) The Benchmark Handbook for Database and Transaction Systems, 2nd edn. Morgan Kaufmann (1993)

14. Rabl, T., Poess, M., Danisch, M., Jacobsen, H.: Rapid development of data generators using meta generators in PDGF. In: Narasayya, V.R., Polyzotis, N. (eds.) Proceedings of the Sixth International Workshop on Testing Database Systems, DBTest 2013, New York, NY, USA, 24 June 2013, pp. 5:1–5:6. ACM (2013). https://doi.org/10.1145/2479440.2479441

15. Sethuraman, P., Reza Taheri, H.: TPC-V: a benchmark for evaluating the performance of database applications in virtual environments. In: Nambiar, R., Poess, M. (eds.) TPCTC 2010. LNCS, vol. 6417, pp. 121–135. Springer, Heidelberg (2011). https://doi.org/10.1007/978-3-642-18206-8_10

16. Taheri, H.R., Little, G., Desai, B., Bond, A., Johnson, D., Kopczynski, G.: Characterizing the performance and resilience of HCI clusters with the TPCx-HCI benchmark. In: Nambiar, R., Poess, M. (eds.) TPCTC 2018. LNCS, vol. 11135, pp. 58–70. Springer, Cham (2019). https://doi.org/10.1007/978-3-030-11404-6_5

17. TPC, T.P.P.C.: TPC-A benchmark specification version 2.0.0 (1999). https://www.tpc.org/TPC_Documents_Current_Versions/pdf/tpca_v2.0.0.pdf

18. TPC, T.P.P.C.: TPC-App benchmark specification version 1.3.0 (1999). https://www.tpc.org/TPC_Documents_Current_Versions/pdf/tpc-app_v1.3.0.pdf

19. TPC, T.P.P.C.: TPC-B benchmark specification version 2.0.0 (1999). https://www.tpc.org/TPC_Documents_Current_Versions/pdf/tpc-b_v2.0.0.pdf

20. TPC, T.P.P.C.: TPC-C benchmark description (1999). https://www.tpc.org/tpcc/default5.asp

21. TPC, T.P.P.C.: TPC-D benchmark specification version 2.1.0 (1999). https://www.tpc.org/TPC_Documents_Current_Versions/pdf/tpcd_v2.1.0.pdf-09-30

22. TPC, T.P.P.C.: TPC-H benchmark description (1999). https://www.tpc.org/tpch/default5.asp

23. TPC, T.P.P.C.: TPC-R benchmark specification version 2.1.0 (1999). https://www.tpc.org/TPC_Documents_Current_Versions/pdf/tpcr_v2.1.0.pdf
24. TPC, T.P.P.C.: TPCx-BB benchmark description (1999). https://www.tpc.org/tpcx-BB/default5.asp
25. TPC, T.P.P.C.: TPCx-HCI benchmark description (1999). https://www.tpc.org/tpcx-HCI/default5.asp
26. TPC, T.P.P.C.: TPCx-IoT benchmark description (1999). https://www.tpc.org/tpcx-IoT/default5.asp
27. TPC, T.P.P.C.: TPCx-V benchmark description (1999). https://www.tpc.org/tpcx-V/default5.asp

# Author Index

R. Nambiar and M. Poess (Eds.): TPCTC 2022, LNCS 13860, p. 149, 2023.
https://doi.org/10.1007/978-3-031-29576-8

Printed in the United States
by Baker & Taylor Publisher Services

Printed in the United States
by Baker & Taylor Publisher Services